The
Holding Room

The
Holding Room

Del Walters

authorHOUSE®

AuthorHouse™
1663 Liberty Drive
Bloomington, IN 47403
www.authorhouse.com
Phone: 1-800-839-8640

Published by AuthorHouse   10/25/2012

ISBN: 978-1-4772-8080-5 (sc)
ISBN: 978-1-4772-8077-5 (hc)
ISBN: 978-1-4772-8079-9 (e)

Library of Congress Control Number: 2012919284

Acknowledgements

This book is dedicated to the angels who surround us all. They are the people who, in our darkest hour, are there to provide comfort and then disappear into the night. They ask nothing in return and only in afterthought become all too clear.

As always my angels are my wife Robin, and my two daughters Taylor and McClaine. I have been blessed with two wonderful parents and a writing support team that reads my each and every word. Jan has always been a stalwart.

It is also dedicated to the déjà vu inside us all.

Prologue

In my Father's house there are many mansions: if it were not so, I would have told you.

I go to prepare a place for you. John 14:2

*G*od has a wicked sense of humor . . . .

It was the sweltering summer of 1963. A little boy, visiting his grandfather, asked the simplest and yet most complex of questions, "what will happen when?"

"Grandfather," he began. "What will happen when you die?"

"If I have lived my life in a good and just manner, I will go to heaven," his Grandfather replied.

"And if not?"

"Then I suppose I will go elsewhere . . ."

"You mean to h-e-double hockey sticks?"

"Precisely," the old man answered. "I will go to hell."

"I hope not," he replied. "Will grandma be there waiting for you in heaven?" the little boy asked looking at the picture of his grandmother that sat on the table next to his grandfather's recliner.

"I hope she will," the older man answered.

Then the little boy studied the picture closer. The woman, his grandmother, died young. She was only fifty or so when the picture was taken, in the prime of her life. He was told she was sick. He believed the cause of her death to be cancer. Still there was something about the photo that didn't make sense. "Grandfather?"

"Yes . . ."

"She will be much younger than you."

"That is correct," his grandfather answered. "She was much younger when she died."

"And *you* look much older . . ."

A pained expression filled the face of the old man as he pondered the thought of a younger woman waiting in heaven for an older, wrinkled, man. Then he remembered what his grandfather told him when they had the same conversation. "I suppose I will go to heaven as a younger man so that she will be able to find me," he replied wisely.

Now the boy was even more perplexed. He studied the photo glancing downward and then up toward his grandfather again and again. "Then how will *I* recognize you?" he asked. "I am used to the way you look now. If you are a young man then when I get to heaven, I will not know what you look like."

"But I will know you," the grandfather answered.

"But what if I too grow older before I die?"

Now it was the grandfather who seemed to be stumped. Indeed the thought of the fine print of dying had escaped him. The countless sermons he listened to as a child and then into adulthood spoke of angelic choirs and a celestial afterlife where families would be reunited to spend eternity together. No one ever explained the fine print that some die young and some die old. Some die intact, and others who are victims of horrible accidents are so disfigured their caskets are closed before their deaths. It seemed that the little boy was on to something. Death, it seemed, was more complicated in practice than on paper. "I guess," the grandfather answered, "That God will sort it all out in the holding room."

"The holding room?"

"Yes," his grandfather explained. "The holding room is a place where we all go to be judged. That is where God sorts out everything including all of the questions you just asked," he added.

"It must be pretty big,' the little boy said softly. As he sat there his eye grew and filled with the wonderment such a room would represent. A place filled with thousands if not millions of people waiting for their chance to get into heaven. Then his thoughts turned to the only barometer a little boy could have of such a gathering, the first day of school. "Must be pretty confusing too . . ."

"God has a wicked sense of humor," the grandfather explained. "And he's pretty smart!"

Chapter one

Time of death

On the morning of July 4th, 2005, Peggy Wilson awoke to die.

She smiled and looked at the clock, which smiled back and was, as always, perched on the wall opposite the foot of her bed. Like everything else in the room, the clock had a story. She remembered how she once tried to remove it, but realized that like all things in life, change is not easy. Underneath the clock, she discovered the bright outline of an object that hadn't been moved in years. The paint around it had grown older and dimmer with her and because repainting the wall was not an option . . . . the clock remained and thus it had its story. And so on this morning, as was the case with every morning until now, the second hand tried to complete its rounds to begin another minute which would lead to another hour which would give way to another humdrum day. But on this day Peggy Wilson would never know the outcome of the journey of the second hand. She had run out of seconds, and of minutes, and of hours, and therefore died not knowing whether the clock stopped before she did, or whether it was the other way around.

Like everything else on the day of your death it mattered little.

At 7:39 a.m., plus or minus a few odd seconds, Peggy Wilson's clock stopped. She closed her eyes forever and died.

The exact time of her death according to the coroner's report was 7:40 a.m. But in reality Peggy Wilson had been ready to die long before that day. She had lived her entire life waiting . . . waiting to be judged for her sins, running from a past that no one knew. She felt she didn't deserve to live. Because of their ignorance, those around her disagreed.

She was the proverbial pillar in her community. She was a deaconess in her church, sang frequently sour notes in the church choir and served meals to the homeless each and every holiday. They were meals that she cooked in her own kitchen, inside her own home, even when her aging, arthritic, hands made it all but impossible. She stayed married to the same man for 58 years, buried a loving husband and raised five successful children and watched them raise fifteen grandchildren. Like most people her age she gave up on keeping count of the great grandchildren.

She did not drink and long ago gave up cursing. The drinking disappeared at the same time her life began to crumble. God knew why . . . it was their secret. And so, on the morning of July 4th at precisely 7:39 and some odd seconds, when the tingling in her hand signaled a massive and unforgiving stroke, and her breathing grew heavy, she raised her eyes upwards and thanked God that the day of her death had finally come. Silently she began to mouth the prayer she prayed every day, *"The Lord is my shepherd, I shall not want,"* and seconds later as the *"table was being prepared in the presence of her enemies"*, she died.

The first to discover her lifeless body was her eldest daughter, "Little Peggy", who also just happened to share her name. At first, as had become the routine, she shook her mother to make sure she wasn't just sleeping. Then she placed a finger underneath her nose to detect even the faintest signs of life. That morning, she realized, no amount of shaking in the world would ever awaken her mother. "Mamma!" she screamed frantically while at the same time dialing the number 911 in her ever present cell phone. "Mamma!" she shouted again. "Please wake up!" she continued shaking Peggy Wilson's lifeless body. Glancing down, she noticed the call on her cell phone had "connected." "Please come quick," she shouted to an uncaring operator, who, as if by routine, cautioned her to remain calm. "Please send someone . . . . Mamma's not breathing, it looks like she suffered a stroke or had a heart attack!" Had she looked closer at her mother, she would have realized it was all ready too late.

The paramedics arrived at 8:10 complaining of rush hour traffic in a city that had none. They bounded the steps with a large orange crash cart, and attempted resuscitation, while at the same time preparing to transport Peggy Wilson to the hospital. "Little Peggy" stood trembling in the corner of the bedroom in the same spot where she had done so as a child. Her husband was now by her side. Sun streaked in from the window next to the bed, in sharp rays that highlighted the dust dancing up on the floor. Peggy Wilson would have hated that! Now, it mattered little. No one would care what type of day it was. No one would care that there was dust to be dusted.

It didn't matter.

Fifteen minutes later, the paramedics placed Peggy Wilson on a gurney, the crash cart underneath, and gently carried her now lifeless body down the steps. Her left arm slipped from beneath the white sheet and dangled off to the side as the cart made its way down the steps. The paramedics already knew the outcome but long ago learned never to give up hope. Hope would be surrendered at a much higher level and a much higher pay grade.

The ashen figure on the gurney was no longer the little girl with the flowing pigtails flapping as she ran up and down the street or raced the other boys with her scooter. There was no longer the smile so full of joy. Gone was the innocence of basement dances underneath amber lights to music that defined her generation. The child, who once threatened six feet, was now shriveled and old. The hazel eyes of her youth had long ago grown dim. Graying and dying, if not already dead, Peggy

Wilson was soon to be no more, "The doors to the ambulance slammed shut as metal met metal and Peggy Wilson would take her last journey on earth.

Although, truth if the truth be known, she was already gone. She was already far far away *"dwelling in the house of the Lord . . . forever"*.

Or so she thought.

3:30 PM

No one is born a bigot, but in less than five minutes Virgil Thompson, a man who once laid claim to being the most hated man in the world without protest, would die one.

He would die a victim of the same hate that he espoused and generated in others. Somewhere between the tolls of the clock in the Bell Tower of Wheeling Central Catholic High School . . . it happened. Somewhere between a speech laced with the hate filled words of "kill" and "niggers", a shot was fired from a gun that would be never be found, by a gunman who would never be seen or sought. Drowned out by the constant ringing of bells the rifle shot escaped Thompson who thought that he had been stung by a bee. Then the small red dot that pierced the white cotton sheets he wore grew larger and larger until it was apparent that Virgil Thompson was bleeding.

A few moments later, he collapsed into a puddle of his own blood which had already started to coagulate, drop by drop, beneath his feet. As he fell to the ground, those he considered closest, his fellow Klansmen, parted ranks and fled in a sea of white sheets and panic. There would be troubles with the law if they waited and most had troubles already. Virgil Thompson, the Grand Dragon of the Ku Klux Klan, would die alone . . . and soon he would die naked and exposed before the world.

"A siren!" he mumbled through heavy, weighted breaths. He heard Sirens. Help was on the way.

The crowd looked on.

It's difficult to gauge pain beneath a hood, or panic in eyes that peered out of peep holes, for that matter, but both were present on the face of a the man who was about to die. In the seconds where life flickered away and death stood at the doorstep, few men stand bold. Virgil Thompson was no different. Instead he ripped away the hood in a last act of defiance. As if to say to the world, *"I am not dead . . . yet,"* and hoping the world cared. Instead the face looking back was the last face expected to see . . . a *black* paramedic. And it was the face of a *black* paramedic who was smiling.

"Clear," he shouted and soon the air was filled with the smell and sound of a charging defibrillator.

By Thompson had already deduced what had happened. Someone fired a shot timed perfectly with the chiming of the clock, but it was too late. The paramedics had already plotted the wrong course. *"I been shot, you black moron,"* Virgil screamed in a voice that fell silent amidst all the commotion.

Seconds later his almost lifeless body leapt from the grounds as thousands of volts of electricity pulsed through his body. A second surge followed producing the same result. At first he closed his eyes in an effort to avoid the pain. It was them, in between the piercing pain and his desperate cries for the paramedics to stop, that he saw it. The paramedic administering the shocks was not only smiling, he was singing. He was mouthing the words to a rap song he knew all too well. The song was about killing "whitey!"

Pausing just long enough to declare, "Still no pulse," the paramedic prepared to charge the paddles once more. Again the pulse fired. Again the body of Virgil Thompson rose from the ground and collapsed once more. Then he pulled out the scissors. "Got to find the source of this bleeding!" the paramedic screamed halfheartedly. It was more for the entertainment of the crowd than any effectual life saving desire, as one pair of scissors cut away the Klansman's outer garb, another paramedic proceeded to tear away his urine stained trousers.

"Just below the heart," Virgil mouthed, still not being heard above the crowd that had begun to gather. *"I was shot just below the heart,"* he continued. Although by now it was clear no one really cared. He was the entertainment, and the paramedics were providing the show.

"He ain't got no d . . . ," a little boy started to say staring at his now shriveled penis, before a loud slap landed on the back of his head, delivered by an equally loud black woman eight times his size. "Watch your mouth!" she declared raising a clenched fist a second time to make sure there was no questioning the first move. The episode prompted the crowd to burst into laughter. More laughter followed as Thompson's trousers were torn away.

Dying and naked, the man who once called himself the Grand Dragon of the KKK was now reduced to an anatomical embarrassing spectacle in the throes of death. Gone were the bravado and the bullhorn that provided volume to a voiceless voice. Gone were the hate, and the anger, and the bitterness that had engulfed him his entire life. Instead, naked before the world was a pathetic man who no longer mattered. It was doubtful he would make tomorrows headlines although his nude shriveled body would become an overnight internet sensation.

No one is born a bigot, but at exactly 3:35, the world watched and laughed as one died. His name was Virgil Thompson.

He lived a life full of hate, and died a hated man.

And no one cared.

He was headed straight to hell . . . or so he thought.

7:30 PM

"Hate" was scheduled to take to the stage at exactly 7:30 PM. It was part of the big July 4th outdoor concert. The concert had been advertised on the black owned radio station in town for weeks and, as such, the event was sold out weeks in advance. Scores of teenagers wearing baggy jeans and exposed underwear, carried coolers filled with booze and packed the outdoor amphitheater. The sun shined brightly, the liquor was consumed and the time was right for "Hate". There were the prerequisite opening acts but no one cared. Then the band played the intro to the song "Hate" made famous, and the dancers gyrated to the music that had become his signature, but Hate was nowhere to be seen.

"Hate's" music, the critics proclaimed, was the perfect amalgamation of black anger against a privileged class they welcomed with open arms. Videos that showed semi nude dancers atop tanks gyrated to music against war. No one made mention of the fact that the women also carried the weapons of choice on the streets, and that "Hate," the video game was an international best seller. "Hate" exploited women and guns and therefore made a comfortable living. There was a market for "Hate" in every demographic category and he took advantage of them all. "Hate" sold well.

"Hate" was a marketing marvel. Standing just over six feet with a chiseled chest and flawless ebony skin, save the obligatory tattoo, "Hate" had legions of fans, male and female and gay. "Hate's" wealth generated a generation of copycats, who sported chiseled chests honed in the best of gyms. What "Hate" drank, they drank. What "Hate" owned, they owned, and what "Hate" ate, they ate. When word hit the streets that "Hate" spent time in jail before becoming a rapper, throngs of young teens wanted to do so as well. It was, they argued, a matter of "street cred."

On this night, however, "Hate" was missing in action.

In fact, "Hate", it seemed, had never arrived. The rapper, known to millions of adoring fans as I-Hate, lay prone on the floor of his dressing room; eyes rolled back, a coke spoon in one hand clutching his heart with his other. White froth poured from his mouth as it quickly became clear he, "Hate", had drowned in his own vomit. Doctors would later reveal that his enlarged heart simply burst. There was a technical term, but no one seemed to care. Not that night.

Instead those who waited until 7:45 to hear him perform began demanding refunds at precisely 7:58. In the world of "Hate" money ruled. By eight o clock the band was no longer playing, the dancers no longer gyrating and the crowd no longer lingered. Perhaps the only excitement came the next morning when it was learned that I-Hate was dead. His name, the papers declared was in reality Isaiah Hawthorne III. He was not born in the inner city as he claimed, but instead in the wealthy confines of suburbia. His entire life was as scripted as his death was unscripted. It seemed that nothing known about "Hate" was true.

The music, which he declared would revive the civil rights movement in rap, was scripted by the same Jewish writers he reviled against. His business manager was named Nathan Schwartz, and his publicist was a Jewish woman named Joni

Olstein. His father married white, his mother hated black. So "Hate" grew up white, lived white, banked white, and died with a white powdery substance in his nose which was the only black thing about him. It was given to him by a member of his all black band.

"Hate's" entire life, the papers would declare, was a lie. Now it mattered little, "Hate" had become a martyr achieving a degree of blackness in death that had escaped him in life. The black community declared the stories about "Hate", were little white lies.

Officially "Hate" died at 7:28 and a few odd seconds.

The seconds mattered little.

Hate was on his way to heaven . . . or so he thought.

Chapter two

T.L. Gray and Sons claimed it had buried all the founding fathers of the small northeast industrial town of Wheeling, West Virginia. Steeped in a tradition of poverty, Wheeling was discovered when coal was king and forgotten when steel was shipped from Japan. When the mines closed and the mills rusted the result were people who closely resembled the local landscape. The colonial style mansion on Main Street, that housed the T.L. Gray and Sons funeral home, towered above every other house in the neighborhood, which had also seen both good times and bad. It was housed between two vacant lots that served as the playground for the town's only junkies.

The pavers that lined the sidewalks bore the name of the old "Wheeling Foundry." It was a depression era project that gave jobs to Wheeling's men and broke their backs in return. Outside the mansion there were six Corinthian columns that framed a large wooden deck that wrapped around the house on three sides. Each was in various shades of a fading shade of white paint. Two lions graced the outer pillar, and they, like T.

L. Gray, had seen better years. Vandals painted the teeth of one lion white, and removed the teeth from the other altogether. On either side of the front door, there were two large wooden rockers, as if those inside had time to enjoy the sunsets that were blocked by the city's only office building. *It* was a law firm that specialized in wills and estate planning.

In fact the only thing certain in Wheeling was death and taxes and the inevitable joke about West Virginia.

Sadly, for T.L. Gray, there was one other thing that was certain, gambling debts. What began as a hundred dollar bet on a horse at neighboring Wheeling Downs soon mushroomed into a full scale addiction. T.L. Gray owed bookies up and down the east coast, and so he literally began robbing both the families of Peter and Paul to pay his gambling debts. It seemed T.L. Gray had a problem. There weren't enough people dying in Wheeling anymore. Wheeling had run out of people. Peter had died and so did Paul and his wife Renee and everyone else along with them.

As a result, T.L Gray, like any other business man had to come up with a way to decrease costs and increase profits. That meant only two things. He either needed more bodies, or come up with a way to keep the bodies he did get, longer. He chose both. "Because of the decomposition of the bodies," he always began in his sales pitch, "It is better to keep the casket closed," he added. He next moved in closer to reveal a smile that contained more gold that his bank accounts contained money.

The truth was, T.L. Gray lost track of who was buried and who was left to rot elsewhere. And so on the afternoon of July 5th, fate and fortune knocked at almost the same time. There were three visitors to Wheeling that day. Two people who arrived were seeking to bury their dead. Business, it seemed, was about to pick up.

"Little Peggy" Wilson arrived first, saying her mother desired a small modest funeral, one that their pocketbooks could afford. Even though T.L. Gray pushed for a much more elaborate "home going" the truth was, her mother left little in the way of monies or personal belongings to pawn. Her plan was to be buried next to her husband of 58 years in the nearby Military Cemetery. There they would spend eternity together. "It's what my mother wanted," "Little Peggy" said sternly. She had been warned by family members that men like T.L Gray would take advantage of their situation and press for the most expensive burial possible. T.L. Gray would argue, she was told, "That this is the last money you will ever spend on your mother." And in fact T.L. Gray did just that. But "Little Peggy" was more than a match for Gray, and had also heard of his gambling addiction. She wanted to make sure that any monies spent were spent on saying goodbye to a mother who had spent a wonderful life on earth and was now ready for her seat in heaven. "There is one other thing," she said softly between tears.

"And that would be . . ."

"Against my wishes," she continued, wiping away the tears with a small handkerchief she kept tucked inside her purse. "My mother's wishes were to be cremated." Had she been more cynical she would have realized that that was indeed a grin breaking the crevices in the normally stern face of T.L. Gray.

For T.L. Gray a cremation was perfect. There would be no need for the customary lying about *open* versus *closed* caskets. His expenses would be minimal and profits would be large. Because of the lobbying efforts of funeral homes like his, people just couldn't be cremated; they first had to have the bodies prepared. As a result, most crematories required that the bodies arrived in a container that either was a casket, or a poor substitute. Some burned the body casket and all. T.L. Gray, as was usually the case, charged for the casket, but simply removed the body once the funeral was over and kept it to be reused. Since few ever attended more than one funeral in a week, his chances of getting caught were slim. When caught he simply informed the family "they chose the same casket as you . . . you should be flattered."

The second time the doorbell rang it was the manager for I-Hate, who wanted nothing in the way of a funeral at such a low-class establishment, and instead wanted the body of the deceased rapper to be prepared for a flight back to L. A., where plans were already being made for a star studded event that would include the Hollywood elite. There was talk it would be televised. When the negotiating was complete it was difficult to determine who got the better of whom, although both men walked away smiling.

The third time the doorbell rang it was unexpected and unwelcome.

"Mr. Gray," the man in the dark blue suit began. He was hiding behind a pair of ever present sunglasses that allowed him to see out but no one to see in.

T.L. Gray estimated that at the time of *his* death he would require an oversized casket. Still, judging by the lack of tobacco stains on his fingers, and his perfect dental work, death was still a long way off. It was an occupational hazard. Everyone who walked through his doors was a potential customer. It was only a matter of time.

"Sir?" the man questioned again.

"Yes sir," T.L. Gray answered nervously. "How might I help you?" It was as if death's hooded harbinger itself had knocked on his door.

"Patrick Hayes," he continued soberly with little or no inflection in his voice. Not even bothering to remove the sunglasses he continued, "FBI!"

The sound of the three letters at the end of the preceding sentenced caused the knees of T.L. Gray to buckle. Like most men who are guilty of everything or something, he wondered why they were there and as such allowed his mind to race through the multitude of scenarios that would send him to prison for quite a long time. And like most men in his position, he played dumb. "And what brings the FBI to my humble enterprise?" he asked politely trying to hide the slight quiver in his voice.

"We have a warrant to search your premises," the agent responded matter-of-factly. "I have nothing to hide," Gray responded, telling the first of many lies. When he lied his lower jaw moved back and forth. At night he grinded his teeth, an indication that he lied even while asleep. "Do I need a lawyer?" At first Gray thought the man said "an army" but the man insisted he said that it was "an option" Gray might want to consider. Still curiosity soon got the best of him. "What might you be looking for?" he asked sheepishly.

"This is a writ of mandamus," he began. "It is the Latin phrase for produce the body. In this case we are seeking the body of Dylan Walsh who died three weeks ago and was placed in your care by the local sheriff's office. You might remember him. He was a skin head. I have a photo here.

T.L. Gray studied the photo. The body of Dylan Walsh lay naked on a coroners table, with tattoos covering almost every inch of his body. Each tattoo bore a message of hate. His head was shaven. Even in death the man on the slab appeared . . . angry. For reasons unknown, panic pierced the normally stoic veneer of T.L. Gray's face. The truth was, he had no idea who Dylan Walsh was nor did he care. If there was a body that was in his funeral home, he hadn't seen it, but he suspected he knew *why* they were there.

It wasn't Dylan Walsh he was worried about; it was about the hundreds of other Dylan Walsh's the sheriff's office had delivered to his funeral home over the years. As he motioned to the body of Virgil Thompson lying on a slab in the mortuary he pointed in a sweeping motion telling the agent, "The sheriff's office delivers hundreds of bodies here each year. They have no money, but we provide them with a proper burial in a pauper's cemetery that the city has established on the outskirts of town near Tunnel Green," he smiled nervously. "It is our Potters Field." His face had the expression on it of a man who had given up on all things proper. Then he added, "There they will rest with the city's other unfortunate souls."

'Then it should be no problem producing the paper work that will show us exactly where Dylan Walsh is buried, now should it?" the agent asked. "You do keep paperwork on all of these bodies . . ."

"Yes sir . . . and no sir, it shouldn't be a problem," Gray replied. "I'll get you all the paperwork you need in a matter of moments. But you must understand, with the holiday and all, my bookkeeper has the day off. In the meantime would you like some tea?"

Chapter three

Kathleen Collins worked the night shift at the Wheeling News and Publisher, and as such had one specialty, obituaries. If it died she wrote about it. Ivy League educated, from rich northeast parents, she saw her trials at the newspaper as down payment on a much larger dream. Her flowing locks of blond hair, and expensive clothes begged of a much once more lavish existence. Plaid pleated skirts bore designer names the rest of Wheeling had never heard of. Her permanent Southern California suntan rivaled any produced by the local tanneries. She was but one "big one" away from leaving her journalistic jail and the illiteracy of Wheeling's low class luminaries and she knew it. They did too. As such, when the phone call came in reporting a scandal at a local funeral home, she saw it as her ticket out of town. Even as the details were being reported she had dreams of phone calls from larger papers in larger cities where people actually *read* the news for its content and not just to see who died. Scandal in this case had three letters; FBI.

"You say they visited T.L. Gray?" she asked, hastily taking notes as she talked. "How many?" she continued scribbling. "What did Gray say?" It was clear her questions outnumbered the answers she was getting from the caller on the other end of the line. It didn't matter. A visit from the FBI in small town American conjured up memories of mobsters hiding out, and big time embezzlers taking advantage of innocent small time folk. She knew it would only be a matter of time before the "big boys" from the larger papers, beginning with the papers in Pittsburgh, descended on the town. Then *her* bylines would be an afterthought. Strangely, the bizarre became even more unusual when a second phone call in as many minutes came into the night desk. This time it was her on again off again boyfriend who worked in construction. "What the hell do you want?" she mouthed looking down at the caller ID. Instinct told her to pick up the call.

"Pack your bags," she said sarcastically. "I'm on my way out of this dump," she added.

"Not before you agree to protect me as your source!" he began.

"You're what?" she asked incredulously.

"Your source," he continued. "I need you to protect me as your source."

"And why should I do that?"

"Because I happen to know that a couple of three letter guys came by the construction company today flashing a rather big check. Seems the big boys plan on doing some digging out the pike by Big Wheeling Creek," he continued.

Big Wheeling Creek flowed from the foothills of the Allegheny Mountains, and fed into the Ohio River which then made its way south to empty to the Mississippi. When the rains fell the trailer parks that lined the creek flooded. When the rains fell hard the trailers disappeared.

Kathleen's mind was racing. Two visits from the FBI in one day in Wheeling. What moments ago seemed impossible was now a reality. There was a story to be had, and she had but one choice. Protocol dictated that she call her editor on the night desk, who as always was at the local bar getting drunk. This time, however, protocol be dammed. She was going to break this 'puppy' and she was going to do it by herself. "Did they say what they were looking for out at Big Wheeling Creek?" she asked.

"Yeah," he answered, "although in not so many words. Seems they handed old man Burress down at the construction company a huge check, with one caveat. He was supposed to keep his mouth shut but you know how that works," he added. "I heard him on the phone with his old lady, talkin' about how they was planning on digging up the land belonging to T.L. Gray. Seems they think he's got some bodies buried out there . . . literally."

Suddenly it all made sense. Unlike her boyfriend, Kathleen knew that T.L. Gray had a crematorium on the grounds near the creek. The land had been in the family for years and when it came time to seek the necessary permits he bribed just about every member of the city council to make sure that it was all kept hush hush. He didn't think the townsfolk would take too kindly to bodies being burned in their back yard and on that account he was probably right.

"One other thing.."

"What's that?"

"If you're planning on heading out there pack a lunch. Traffic is backed up all the way back to the pike," he replied.

"Why?"

"Seems some lady tried dodging a dear and wound up running smack dab into a tree, you know that big oak that sits in the parking lot of the first Presbyterian Church?"

"Yeah . . . I know the one . . . is she okay?"

"Nope! Here's the story. Seems one of the feds was in the car in front. He missed the deer but she didn't have time to react. Totaled the car and took a big hunk out of the tree. When I went by they had her body on a stretcher with the tarp over it . . . if you catch my drift."

"Oh . . ."

"Just take it easy," he answered. "A lot of strange stuff has been happening around here lately. I don't want you getting caught up in something bigger than your paper can handle . . ."

The sudden sense of compassion was touching. "Okay . . . you're my source," she said nervously, providing her boyfriend with some semblance of shield protection. "But if you breathe a word of this to anyone else I'll kill you," she tacked on for good measure. "Especially that slut Nancy you sleep with on the side," she added.

"Nancy . . . ."

"Don't go there," she said defiantly. "You forget I work for the town's only newspaper."

Chapter four

T.L Gray was suddenly up to his eyeballs in controversy and meeting people he had never seen before and some, for that matter, he hoped never to see again. The first group to arrive was the team of lawyers representing the estate of I-Hate. They were the first to see the headlines in the local paper and wanted to make sure there would be no delays in getting the body of the rapper where it needed to be on time. There were, after all, memorial services that had already been scheduled. They were willing to pay whatever it took to make sure there were no delays. Not sure whether he could deliver on his promise, T.L took their money and then kept his distance, preferring to let the Feds sort it all out.

His own lawyer, Reggie Katzenbaum, who also played tight end on the high school football team when they were in school together, advised him to say nothing. Still Katzenbaum kept up with just about every movement of the FBI, providing more information that any lawyer should. He wanted to be, "cooperative," he said. The truth was, he knew that his handwriting was on much of the paperwork that the Feds would be looking at pertaining to the funeral home. Katzenbaum knew the system. He knew that if things got too hot, he would cut a deal to testify against his client, in this case T.L. Gray, in exchange for lenience and possibly keeping his legal license as well.

Then there were the Feds. When Agent Haynes showed up the next morning wearing coveralls and digging boots T.L. Gray became even more concerned. Reviewing his paperwork was one thing, but these men looked like they were going to be doing much much more. They were digging for more than information and he had far too many bodies in his closets. That's when Katzenbaum appeared out of nowhere looking as if he had seen a ghost.

"Have you read this thing?" he said panting as if he had just run a marathon.

"Yeah they want to go through my books," Gray said, acting as if he had read the document when in fact he hadn't "Said something about a writ of mandelay . . ."

"Mandamus you asshole. It's Latin for hand over the body but, in this case, they're not looking for *a* body, they're looking for *bodies*," he added.

"Then they shouldn't have much of a problem," Gray replied. "Just look around you.'

"Not here you dumbass . . . . at the farm!"

Gray felt his hear quicken. The thought of federal agents fanning out across the farm was enough to send his heart into cardiac arrest. Looking over his paperwork for bodies at the funeral home was one thing, but the farm was a completely different matter. The farm was five hundred acres of trouble waiting to be tilled in eight foot increments. The farm was a one way ticket to prison.

"Do you have any idea how many bodies there might be?" Katzenbaum whispered hoping not to be heard by the Feds.

"No . . ." Gray began to answer sheepishly.

"Ten . . . fifteen . . . ."

"Hundreds . . ."

"Are you shittin me?"

"I wish I was." Gray replied. "I wish I was."

"How in the hell did you get so many bodies?" Katzenbaum asked, causing the agents to turn around and then lowering his voice accordingly. He whispered, "Hundreds?"

"Let's just say I had a lot of gambling debts and had to go outside the region!"

Chapter five

The right Reverend Eugene Kinney was sitting in his study reading the headlines. Kinney was the pastor of the First Baptist Church of Wheeling. The church was neither. There were many other First Baptist churches in town, and it was not in Wheeling. Instead it was in the suburb of Warwood, which was just six miles up the road north of town and, as far as society was concerned, in another world. It was also more of an abandoned storefront than a church and as such looked like it could double for a furniture storeroom when not being used by parishioners. There were sixteen rows of ten seats, each with the name, "T.L. Gray Funeral Home" stenciled across the back in black paint. Each was aligned to the rows of splintered wood on the floor. On many of the seats, the T.L. had been worn away and only Gray remained. On each seat there were small paper fans with wooden spindles provided by the same funeral home with the same name written across the back. On the front there was the image of a loving family that bore a resemblance to no one who had ever lived or would live in Wheeling. The fans had so much graffiti written on them, the kids in almost all of the pictures had full grown beards. On any given Sunday there were fewer than twenty parishioners, the most devoted of whom was Peggy Wilson.

As he read the papers he felt better about convincing Little Peggy that any funeral would take months. Reverend Kinney also managed to convince "Little Peggy" that there should first be a memorial service so that her mother's memory could be honored and a funeral later. Reverend Kinney also saw the possibility of double the money from twice as many people attending both the memorial service and subsequent funeral, as ever worshiped in his church on Sunday. He was also trying to cash in on his new found notoriety.

Three weeks earlier, it was he, Reverend Eugene Kinney, who gained national attention by first publically announcing, and then burning several hundred copies of the Koran. He told the assembled press that they were given to him by various parishioners from around the country who shared his radical views. But the truth was he purchased them out of his own pocket to make for a bigger bond fire. The event captured attention from around the world and the press descended on tiny Wheeling like a swarm of Biblical locusts looking for the next crop to destroy. There were satellite trucks with cameras in front blocking traffic along the town's main road. Reporters filled the local hotels and motels and emptied the liquor from local bars telling stories of wars gone by.

The local bum, turned entrepreneur printed T-shirts with the right Reverend Kinney emblazoned on them, proclaiming that he was a "Christian Soldier." The local Sheriff's office, which had to provide security for Reverend Kinney because of the numerous death threats he had received after announcing the stunt, was certain that Kinney was getting a percentage of every shirt sold. He was the darling of TV networks on the right, and scorned by those on the left. He was famous for more than fifteen minutes. He also drew the wrath of Peggy Wilson.

It was Peggy Wilson who argued that hate begat hate and she was right. Despite protests from as far away as the White House and others in Washington, Reverend Kinney stood firm with his plans. Plans that drew international condemnation and a sharp rebuke from the Secretary of Defense who argued doing so would endanger the troops stationed in Afghanistan. Religious leaders from all walks of life signed a petition begging Kinney to reconsider in the name of the God he professed to represent. Peggy Wilson met with him privately and issued the same plea. Still, she stood alongside the rest of the congregation as the cameras rolled and the Korans burned. At first the fires flickered out, but as dusk set in, they roared. At the crescendo of the flames, Reverend Kinney addressed the assembled reporters and said he was doing "God's work."

There was no reaction from God.

Chapter six

The body of Virgil Thompson lay unattended in the funeral home along with the other bodies that T.L. Gray took in that week. Even though the Bureau's work had not reached the tedious stage, the week was not without incident. A photographer from a tabloid magazine managed to sneak in the funeral home to take photographs of the Klan Grand Dragon's naked body. The photos were subsequently splashed across the front pages of a magazine few outside the community of hate ever read. Circulation was low because fewer still could read. It stated simply, *"The Naked Truth."* Only the FBI was upset, more concerned that their perimeter had been breached than about any violation of Thompson's privacy. The legions that Thompson claimed to represent made no claims on his body and stayed as deep underground as humanly possible. There were no kin, no loved ones, no one who laid claim to a life unspent.

In the days since his death Thompson's body took on a pale shade of gray, complimented by the large crimson, "Y" shaped, scar carved into his chest by an overeager Medical Examiner. The M.E. told the assembled reporters he wanted to make sure he knew the "exact" cause of death. In the end the ruling was as anticlimactic as the rally that preceded Thompson's death. Still, it required the prerequisite press conference, and the Medical Examiner felt more than willing to oblige.

"The exact cause of death," the Medical Examiner began, after waiting for reporters to settle, "was death by gunshot, and complications from a heart attack." The truth was, there was

no heart attack, but a deal had struck long ago between the Medical Examiner and his high school buddies on the rescue squad that he would clean up their mistakes. In this case, the cleanup included the fact that Thompson had been shocked senseless by the two paramedics who, quite simply, couldn't stand his sight. He had been shocked so many times, the Medical Examiner discovered, that the tiny metal bullet exited the body courtesy one of the paddles used to shock him. Thompson, he found, could have survived the gunshot but not the assault that accompanied his care.

He was destined to die.

Chapter seven

" I guess they all get what they deserve," a solemn Suleiman Muhammad declared after reading the articles on the subsequent FBI search of the farm of T.L. Gray. "An eye for an eye," he continued, folding the paper and placing it atop a stack of otherwise worthless reading. "And they think *we* are dangerous,' he concluded.

Muhammad spent most of his life in relative obscurity. His landlord once complained of the sparseness of his apartment to the FBI in the days and months following the September 11th Terrorist Attacks, but it was quickly determined that Al Qaida had no designs of small towns like Wheeling. Suleiman's only crime was that he was a Muslim in a city of Irish and Italian Roman Catholic bigots who hated any and all things that looked different. They prayed to a God that demanded that they partake of his body once a month, Suleiman Muhammad faced east five times a day on a prayer mat that had been handed down from generation to generation since it's return from Mecca decades earlier. Still, *he* was considered the extremist.

Muhammad, like his father, and his father's father before him, sold hot dogs on Wheeling's Plaza. Their store bore proud pictures of an immigrant empire that began as a small metal cart and mushroomed into a prime spot on a dying piece of real estate. It was the American dream 'Muslim' style. Sporting the stereotypical turban and unshaven face that gave way to an unyielding beard, the now be-speckled Suleiman faced more than his share of heckles from high school kids who had already reached their zenith in life. He was their entertainment, they were his curse. But like all men, Muhammad had a tipping point, a point of no return where anger, fused with hate, became actionable.

Today was that day.

That morning, facing east, and following his prayers, Muhammad decided his faith demanded retaliation. "Something," he thought, "must be done!" The right reverend Eugene Kinney insulted his religion, his prophet, his Koran. Therefore the right Reverend Eugene Kinney must pay! It was, Muhammad reasoned, "an eye for an eye!"

Never even a hunter let alone a terrorist, Muhammad found more than his fair share of explosives. He told the local hardware store owner that he had a stump that needed to be removed from his farm on the outskirts of town. He needed "black powder," he reasoned, "lots of it." Because harsh economic times demand few answers, he left the store with enough power to destroy the hardware store itself, no questions asked.

Then, fashioning a series of crudely made pipe bombs out of ½ inch pieces of PVC tubing and some black tape he headed to the church were Reverend Kinney was set to deliver the eulogy of one Peggy Wilson, according to the Wheeling News and Publisher. The paper also pointed out that the body would be eulogized in absentia because of the growing scandal at T.L Gray's funeral home. It was a polite way of saying that there would be no body to bury until the FBI concluded its matters in Wheeling. The paper provided the time, place and list of all the attendees but Muhammad was only interested in one. He was only interested in the right Reverend Eugene Kinney.

The service was scheduled to begin at 10:00 and so at 9:25 Muhammad stood on the opposite side of the street as the mourners, including "Little Peggy" began to pour into the tiny storefront church. Outside, Reverend Kinney greeted each and every person who entered, making sure that they knew that, "they could return Sunday for some good old fashioned preaching!"

No one noticed that Muhammad, perched under a tree on the opposite side of the street, appeared much larger and much thicker than normal. Fewer still noticed that he was sweating profusely and wearing a large woolen coat on what was to become one of the hottest days of the year. Fewer still noticed his eyes darting wildly from side to side, or saw him walking across the street directly toward the right Reverend Eugene Kinney. In fact he wasn't noticed at all, until it was too late.

In the instance between decision and indecision, Muhammad found himself focused on the morning prayers he had just completed. Burning the Koran was wrong, but so was killing out of revenge. It wasn't his Muslim values that guided him at this point; it was a curious mix of American right and wrong taught in the most elementary of school lessons. It was the tiny voice inside his head that was telling him what he was about to do was wrong. Still, as he gripped the small crudely made triggering device, he knew that indecision would once again be replaced by anger and in that moment he would strike.

Or would he?

Chapter eight

Reverend Kinney was ushering in the stragglers and about to close the doors to the church, when he caught a fleeting image of Suleiman Muhammad approaching out of the corner of his eye. His mind was already preparing to repeat the invitation to next Sunday's services but his body was telling him he was in danger. All he could see were the eyes of the man who was about to become his assassin. They were eyes that framed a face, hidden by a beard, that seemed to be smiling!

Muhammad's footsteps were hurried, as he was less than fifteen feet from Reverend Kinney and closing in fast. "In the name of the Honorable Elijah Muhammad I wish to ask you why?" he said in a demanding tone.

Reverend Kinney, who told reporters that he was prepared to fight and die for his religious beliefs seemed ready to do *neither* and instead attempted to quickly close the door before Muhammad's arrival. It was too late, not that the door would have done any good anyway. In what he assumed would be the last moments in his life on earth he uttered what he also assumed would be his last words. "God . . . help!"

God was not listening.

As Suleiman Muhammad extended his hand toward Reverend Kinney a shot from an FBI sniper rifle rang out. There was nothing in the way of any other sound. There was nothing to cause the crowds that gathered inside to hurry outdoors or press their faces towards the windows. There was only the sight of Muhammad's body collapsing to the ground, and the spray of pink that accompanied the arrival of the sniper's shell.

The Bureau, Kathleen Cunningham would report exclusively, had been tracking the movements of Muhammad for quite some time. When the purchases of such large sums of black powder were recorded, it appeared that a "sleeper cell" had been activated. In truth it was the ranting of Reverend Kinney that caused the Bureau to take a second look at complaints about Muhammad. Acting on those complaints, the agency's Rapid Response Team was called into action. Right before the funeral, a sniper had been positioned on the rooftop of small Victorian house less than a block away. The single shot from the high powered rifle felled Muhammad just as he was about to detonate the bomb. Reverend Kinney's life had been spared . . . or so it seemed.

In the confusion that followed, no one noticed Reverend Kinney's body slumped in the doorway of the First Baptist Church. Nor would anyone hear his muffled pleas for help until it was too late. No one heard his last cries for help. No one saw the pained expression on his face as his eyes recorded their last moments on earth. No one cared.

The man, who was accused of not having a heart, had suffered a massive heart attack.

Chapter nine

Sunday's edition of the Wheeling News and Publisher carried the headlines, *"FBI Scuttles Terrorist Attack on Wheeling!"* There were photos of the prone body of Suleiman Muhammad on the ground where he had been shot. There were also photos of his smiling face pulled from a profile they did on his hot dog restaurant years earlier in a small box in the corner of the larger photo. The local sheriff, who was clueless to the entire episode, bragged that it was he who tipped off the FBI to Suleiman's movements. He also warned of other sleeper cells in the city and fingered just about every other ethnic group that called Wheeling home.

For its part, the FBI said nothing and declared the case an episode of a single "lone wolf" bent on revenge against an extremist minister. The agency said there was nothing in the background of Muhammad to suggest that he was acting in concert with other extremists domestically or otherwise. He did not travel overseas or worship inside any radical temples where extremist views were espoused. What the FBI didn't report was that there were internal concerns that Muhammad wasn't going to detonate any bombs, because the bombs were dummy's. There were also concerns that the sniper pulled the trigger prematurely. The media had a different take on the issue.

TV talk shows declared the assassination poetic justice. Ministers said that God had the last word on the right Reverend Eugene Kinney who now occupied a slab on the 'cold table' wedged in between tables bearing the bodies of Virgil Thompson and Peggy Wilson. There he lay, awaiting word from the FBI as to when they might be laid to rest.

Chapter ten

"Sir," the fresh faced deputy in charge began. "We have an issue." Sean Hanlon was just out of the academy in Quantico, Virginia and, as such, found himself stationed in the Siberia of assignments, Wheeling, West Virginia. Still, like all freshmen feds, he believed his case was the most important and pressing in the nation.

"And what might that be Agent Hanlon?" Agent Haynes answered.

"We have bodies' sir . . . bodies that are beginning to pile up . . . what should we do with them?"

"We?"

"We'll sir. The director of the funeral home is telling the townspeople that he can't burry their loved ones until the Bureau releases the bodies ."

"That's a crock of . . ." Agent Haynes fired back. "What that lazy asshole won't tell the townspeople is that he lacks the funds to pay for their loved ones to be prepared! Now he wants to pin it on the Bureau!"

"Sir," Agent Hanlon continued. "I am aware of what *you* are saying and what *he* is doing. The problem is sir . . . it is a Bureau problem. He lacks the funds . . . and we are stuck in the position of tying this up in the courts while the bodies rot. Need I point out that one of those bodies belongs to the rapper . . . ."

""I Hate" . . . I know!" Agent Haynes added. "Now I know how he got his name. I hear from his representatives each and every day. It seems they are planning a big shin dig in Hollywood!"

Like all junior agents, Agent Hanlon had a plan even before he entered the room to present the problem. "Sir?" he began. "I think we might be able to come up with a solution that might keep all interested parties happy . . ."

"And that would be?"

"We'll it seems that everyone involved wants to have their loved ones cremated. All, that is, save Virgil Thompson the Klan Grand Dragon and he doesn't have a will on record and no one has come forward to claim his body. The rapper, on the other hand, could be a problem. His group wants his remains delivered to Hollywood. But there's a problem with that . . ."

"Now what?"

"Seems the local Medical Examiner didn't do a good job on the autopsy and T.L. Gray failed to properly embalm him . . . ."

"And?"

42

"And he's a mess sir . . . and I really mean a mess!" Agent Hanlon continued. "He stinks!"

"Stinks?"

"Yes sir, he is stinking the entire joint up . . . sad to say that he's worse off than any of the others. When T.L. Gray ran out of prep tables he just left the body on a folding table in the back of the room. Fluids started to drain and . . . we'll let your imagination do the rest . . ."

"I'd rather not," Agent Haynes continued. "Can you convince his people that it would be in their best interests that "I-Hate" or whatever his name is be cremated?"

"I'm already ahead of you on that sir," Agent Hanlon added. "All I need is your signature here."

Chapter eleven

Within a week, the talk of a terrorist attack in Wheeling was quickly supplanted by stories of the latest torrid affair between a member of the City Council and the equally powerful School Board. That was until Kathleen Collins decided to cash in on her fifteen minutes of fame.

The headlines said it all:

"OPEN GRAVES UNDRE LAND OWNED BY T.L.
GRAY FUNERAL HOME!
HUNDREDS OF BODIES DUMPTED!"

Speaking exclusively to Collins, Agent Haynes said that T.L. Gray, haunted by gambling debts, accepted bodies from overflowing crematoriums in nearby cities and in return provides the ashes of the dead and missing on a body in, body out basis. Haynes said because the bodies were in various states of decomposition a proper burial for many of the deceased was not possible. FBI Forensics teams were brought in from as far away as California to begin the grim process of identifying the dead. He said he believed many were simply indigents from nearby cities and that they would be cremated and buried in a pauper's cemetery on the outskirts of town.

For her part, Kathleen Collins used the most of her fifteen minutes appearing on several national talk shows, never once forgetting to remind viewers that it was she, "who broke the story." In typical media fashion the small tag line that ran underneath the screens told the story in a single phrase, "FBI Admits Grave Concerns!" In the interest of justice, the bureau announced most, if not all of the bodies would be cremated and given a proper burial.

By now the tiny mortuary of T.L Gray was filled with the bodies of Peggy Wilson, Virgil Thompson and now the right Reverend Eugene Kinney. There was also the badly decaying corpse of rapper "I-Hate" and beside him Suleiman Muhammad the terrorist. Like the others found at the farm, the bureau announced that by special agreement, they would be cremated and memorialized elsewhere.

Chapter twelve

Awakenings

P eggy Wilson was the first to die.
She was also the first to awaken.

The surroundings were strange.

There was no bright light as she had expected. Instead there was only a darkness that was darker than anything she had ever seen before. It was as if the darkest sky yielded nothing in the way of light from the faintest of stars. It was blacker than the blackest black she had ever seen. It was cold and damp. To add to the confusion there was a strange physical sensation she had never before felt and the troubling thoughts it produced. The sensation was both exciting and sexual, coming from the area inside her groin. Suddenly she knew exactly what it was, and the thought of what it *might* be caused her to repulse.

"An erection!" she cried out with the horror of a woman who thought all such thoughts to be pornographic at best. "What the . . . hell," she screamed. Glancing downward, and daring to take a look, it appeared her first thoughts were indeed correct. At first she was afraid to touch it, let alone continue to look at what was now becoming obvious. The bulge in her pants left little doubt as to what it was. It was, "An erection?"

But she was a woman, or so she thought.

Almost as startling was the response to her question. It came out of the darkness. The voice that answered came from a person across the room, one that she had not seen when she first awakened. She found it hard to discern just who was doing the talking. There was a faint outline of a person, but because of the intense darkness it was difficult to make out the features. She was sure it was the voice of woman and quite certain it sounded vaguely familiar. That's when she saw the body from which the voice emanated. It did indeed come from a woman and it was a woman who was extremely familiar. It was her, or at least it looked like her!

But if it was *her*, then who was this strange person nursing an erection in the body of a man looking back. Peggy Wilson was speechless and confused and excited.

"Yes, let's just say that things are a little confusing at first," the voice coming from her body replied.

"Confusing!" she screamed. "It's an erection! How can you explain an erection in an 84 year old woman," she screamed. "I know what one looks like . . . now, as to what one feels like that's a different subject!" As she continued she noticed the deepness in what she believed to be her voice. A voice as foreign as the body she now occupied.

"You *were* an 84 year old woman," the voice replied. Your *body* still is. That is the body that I now occupy. You *spirit* is elsewhere. Based on the fact that you are speaking for Peggy Wilson, it would appear that *your* spirit is in another body . . . *his* body."

"So let me see if I have this right. You are in my body and I am in someone else's body?"

"The body of a man to be correct . . . ."

Peggy Wilson took a few moments to digest what had just been stated so matter-of-factly. "Am I dead?"

"Very!" the voice replied.

"Are you?"

"That would seem to be the case," the voice replied.

"God!"

"Yes."

At first it seemed like a bad dream but it was too real. She remembered dying and even hearing the voices of the paramedics as they tried to revive her. She remembered the anguished cries of her daughter "Little Peggy.' She remembered it all. And then as she had been told so many times before, she remembered walking toward the light. But that is where what seemed to be a dream turned into a nightmare.

That's when she remembered the one thing she wished to forget . . . waking up inside the body of a man . . . the horror of waking up with an erection! She was afraid to touch it, afraid to talk about it and afraid to even move.

Taking a moment to survey her surroundings she saw what appeared to be a number of people frozen in place, and yet each seemed to be somehow illuminated. It was as if she walked into a museum of people, each with a small strand of light positioned directly overhead. Each person was immortalized in the manner in which they died. Most of their faces were unrecognizable, except for the Klansman. She recognized his face from the various news accounts she'd seen on TV in the days before her death. His face was unmistakable. His was a face of hate. She was certain he was headed straight to hell and feared she had followed him.

"Is this heaven . . . or hell?" she asked with an almost disappointed tone in her voice. She expected angelic choirs and people with wings floating on clouds of unbelievable happiness. She expected harps, flutes, God! She didn't expect to see the Grand Dragon of the KKK. She also didn't expect she would awaken in heaven with an "erection."

"No . . . this isn't heaven . . . not yet . . ."

"Yet?"

"*Yes* . . . it's not heaven, and *no* not yet."

"Is this what I'm going to look like if and when I get there?" she asked glancing down at her still bulging crotch.

"We'll that depends," the voice answered calmly. "It Seems a bunch of you were cremated together."

"So you're saying I'm going to heaven or hell as a man?"

"I wouldn't get too upset. It's a small technicality."

"Technicality!" she belted out. "Small? I'd say *this* is a rather large technicality to say the very least!"

"We'll it's small for me. You see your ashes got mixed up with the ashes of the others you see around you and, so it seems, your spirit as well. That's why you have all of *your* thoughts and memories in someone else's body. The body you now reside in once belonged to someone else . . ."

"And don't you think *he* might want it back?"

"Not anytime soon . . ."

"Oh I take it he's dead too?"

"Precisely!" the voice said calmly. "Don't worry . . . ."

"Don't worry?"

"Yes . . . don't worry . . . it will all work out if and when you get to heaven," the voice answered.

"If and when," Peggy Wilson heard. "You're saying if and when?"

"That is correct. You must understand that heaven has never been guaranteed. Call it what you will . . . judgment day . . . the day of reckoning . . . the last supper . . . . there are many descriptions for what happens before you are allowed to enter into the Kingdom of Heaven. I warned you time and time again that this day would come and yet like most people you waited until the end to atone for your sins. Think about it. You fill out more forms to take out a mortgage on your house. Heaven is getting crowded. We have to do some last minute fact checking before everyone gets in . . . ."

"Checking?"

"Yeah . . . it used to be real easy. Nowadays there's an entire wing in heaven working on the social media alone, Facebook pages, friend requests . . . sexting! Don't get me started on sexting. Let a woman into heaven the other day and then the photos surfaced . . . . wow!!!!"

"Oh I see . . . I guess it isn't as easy as it used to be back in your time, "she began before catching herself in mid-sentence.

"My time is eternity," the voice interrupted. "Let's just say for every blessing I bestow upon humanity something new crops up. I gave you fire to cook with and you invented flaming arrows. The wheel led to the chariot. Dynamite became a bomb and atomic energy led to the cold war. The internet has been a story in and of itself."

"I see . . ."

"Before that, there was TV. Life was simple when people spoke to each other, or wrote letters. There was a paper trail and life . . . and death was a lot simpler. You had a permanent record."

Peggy Wilson took a moment to let it all soak in. Then she looked down at her hands as she studied her new body. They were unmistakably male and they were tattooed. *"Tattoo's . . . I have tattoos,"* she mused. *"I hate tattoos!"* But they weren't any ordinary tattoos.

Across her fingers, on one hand, a single word, "H-A-T-E" was spelled out in crudely formed dark green letters. As her eyes scanned upwards she realized her arms were no different. There were thousands of tattoos on her newly discovered body, each telling a different story. Words like R-A-P-E with corresponding scenes in a tapestry of terror. "Whose body is this?" she asked.

"In due time," came the response from the voice. "You will understand it all in due time."

Suddenly Peggy Wilson began to laugh. It was a nervous laugh at first that started as a chuckle and became more verbose as it grew in intensity.

"This is funny to you?"

Peggy Wilson reached down and pulled outward the waistband of the rather baggy pair of pants she was now wearing. There was no belt to keep them from falling to the ground, and a pair of boxers that she assumed hadn't seen a laundry in days. Glancing downward she looked upon her new body for the first time. There was indeed an erection down there!

"Happens every morning," the voice replied. "You'll get used to it."

"So you mean I'm going to spend the rest of my *death*, as a man?" she asked.

"That," the voice replied, "is up to you."

Chapter thirteen

A s he was the second to die, Virgil Thompson was the second to awake.

As was the case with Peggy Wilson, the room around him was dark and damp and smelled of old socks. It was a musty smell that resembled the smell that emanated from an old house has that hadn't been opened in quite some time. It smelled of wet plaster and mold mixed. And as was the case with Peggy Wilson, Virgil Thompson noticed the small lights cast on each of the others who were in the room. None of the frozen figurines appeared even vaguely familiar.

Peggy Wilson had rejoined the frozen. There was the right Reverend Eugene Kinney, Suleiman Muhammad . . . and himself! There standing frozen in a corner of the room staring back at him, was a man who bore the sheets and hoods that symbolized the hatred that had become synonymous with his life. As he moved in for a closer look he realized the man bore more than a just resemblance.

IT WAS HIM!

As he moved even closer still and reached out to touch the lifeless figure before him he realized one other thing. *He* was not *himself!* If that was him, who was he? In that moment of confusion he realized something was terribly wrong and it was about to get worse. As he examined the fingers reaching out to make contact with the man who appeared to be him, he realized he had become his own worse nightmare. The fingers belonged to a black man. that could only mean that if the fingers were black, then he was black!

"How do you like your new body?" the voice asked.

Startled, Thompson looked around the room to see where the voice came from. He was even more surprised to learn it came from his body, or at least the body that looked like him. Someone was inside his body, speaking with his voice. He stumbled backwards in disbelief.

"What the . . ." he began.

"Hell?" the voice asked.

Thompson or whoever he was frozen. The word "hell" suddenly took on new meaning. He had wondered for years whether he would go to heaven and had become convinced over the years that he would not. Still the thought of spending an eternity in 'hell' as a *black* man seemed cruel beyond imagination. Then it dawned on him, if he was a black man, then who was inside *his* body.

"Sucks don't it?" the man inside *his* body asked sarcastically. "Sucks you bein' me and me bein' you," then struggling he continued. "Let me tell you this body really dose suck," he added. "What-d'ya smoke . . . two packs a day? I can barely breathe!"

"Three," Thompson replied. "And if you don't mind me asking, who in the hell are you or should I say who in the hell am I?"

"Your given name was Isaiah Hawthorne, but the world knows you as someone else altogether," the voice began by way of explanation. "You might have heard his songs. You are now in the body of the singer who was best known as I Hate," he added.

"I hate? What type of name is that?'

"It's a stage name you idiot. Because you're too stupid to figure this all out, I'll cut to the chase.

Seems when all of you in this room were cremated your remains got all mixed up. I read someplace where funeral homes don't really burn all of the bodies separately. Too much money involved in heating up and cooling down the oven so to speak. The end result, you got mixed up being baked. That means your spirit is in the body of I hate, and I get to float from body to body."

"But I ain't no nigge . . . ."

"Nigger?" came back the response from the voice. "You may not think you're a nigger but from where I'm standing you are a black man for now . . ."

"Okay, okay . . ."

". . . . and I hate to say it but it seems I got the worst of this deal for the moment. Your body stinks, literally, and his looks like it suits you just fine. If you could adjust your attitude . . . ."

"So how do we fix this?' Thompson inquired.

"You don't, I do. When and if I please,' the voice replied.

Taking a moment to explore his new body Thompson suddenly realized he now moved with an ease in death he had not known in life. Gone were the jerky, pronounced movements of a man who battled arthritis in the last throes of his life. Instead this body seemed to float across the room and at times appeared almost instantaneously where needed.

In addition the voice coming from his old body was not his voice. It was a voice he had heard before time and time again. It was, he believed, the voice he had heard over and over again in his head.

"Are you . . ."

"God?" The voice answered. "I get that a lot, and the answer is yes."

"So am I in heaven?" Thompson asked shyly, afraid of what the answer might be.

"If you were in heaven the word *"nigger"* would have never pursed your lips or mine either for that matter. We don't use such words in heaven."

"Then where in the hell am I?" Thompson snapped back, impatiently seeking an answer.

"Fortunately for you, you are neither in heaven or hell," the voice answered. "If you were you'd already be headed south . . . if you catch my drift."

"No shit . . ." he stammered. He then thought for a second. "Excuse me?" he offered up realizing that he had just cursed in front of God. "I didn't mean to use swear words . . ."

"No offense taken," came back the response. "Had this actually been heaven there might have been a lightning strike."

"Really?"

"No . . . just kidding. We don't do that anymore!"

"Thank God . . . I mean thank You."

"You're welcome."

"So what's next," Thompson asked with the innocence of a child expecting a gift at Christmas time when he knew he had been bad. "Am I going to get into heaven?"

"That depends," the voice replied.

"On what," Thompson asked.

"On which Virgil Thompson presents himself next, the hate monger or the child I once knew growing up in Moundsville."

"Oh you mean *him*," Thompson answered almost as if he were embarrassed by the child the voice referred to.

"He is all that matters," the man answered. "If you think there is a place for a Klan Grand Dragon in heaven then I have some *"swamp water in hell"* to sell you," the voice continued. "Get it . . . swamp water in hell?"

"I get it!" Thompson replied.

"That little boy is the only chance you have left at salvation. I would suggest you figure out how to get him back and perhaps then *you're* gone," the voice added.

"But he was so . . ."

"Weak?"

"Yeah . . . . how is it that you always finish my . . ."

"Sentences . . . think about it. It will come to you soon."

Chapter fourteen

T he right Reverend Eugene Kinney awoke next facing Suleiman Muhammad. Muhammad seemed to be frozen in place in the moments before attempting to detonate the explosive device he had crudely fashioned. The mere sight of the man he believed killed him caused panic to spread once more. It was the last thing he remembered in the moment before everything went black. As such he had not yet time to process his panic. Again he felt the tightness in his chest but this time, it went away as quickly as it came. Then he remembered what happened after the pain. He remembered frantically calling out for help. He remembered the fog . . . . he remembered watching as everyone attended to Muhammad and yet there he was dying, crying out for help.

No one came.

He remembered dying.

"Am I . . ."

"Dead?" the voice answered, coming from the body of Muhammad who suddenly came to life. "Yes."

"So this is . . . ?"

"Heaven . . . or hell . . . depending on where you thought you were going to wind up? No," the voice replied.

"Then where am I?" he asked.

"Call it *"The holding room"*," the voice answered.

"Holding room?'

"Yes . . . a holding room. You're not quite anywhere just yet. You are neither here, nor there. You are in between. You have one last chance to make it into either heaven or hell, but this time it is truly your last chance. There are no do-over's from this point forward."

"Are you . . . ."

"God? Yes."

"But that's impossible . . . God wouldn't try to kill me," Reverend Kinney replied, realizing that in this case, the voice of God was coming from the body of Suleiman Muhammad.

"God didn't," the voice answered. "Man did and man succeeded . . . ."

"But you're the man who . . . ."

"Tried to kill you? Sucks don't it." the voice replied bringing forth a full dose of sarcasm.

"This doesn't make sense . . . ."

"Hypocrisy rarely does. How many sermons have you preached telling parishioners that I created man in my own image," the voice answered. "Did you think that only *you* were supposed to look like me, or people who looked like you? To blacks I am black and to whites I am white and so on and so forth. Unlike you, I don't discriminate. I see the beauty in all living things."

"It's not that I was discriminating," and then Reverend Kinney froze in mid sentence, fearing his next words might be used against him. Logic set in. "I mean we all discriminate . . ."

"I don't," the voice replied.

"I mean all men do . . ." Reverend Kinney answered.

"I know," the voice answered. "That's part of the problem with mankind. You fail to see the *"me"* in *"you"*. Instead you only see the *"you"* in *"you"* and that has led to more wars in *my* name than you can imagine. Bigotry is a tool of, well, the other side. So is hate. I am the God of love. I left you a book explaining all of this. You know . . . the Bible . . . a few hundred pages . . . . lots of begats . . . . didn't you read it?"

"Of course," Reverend Kinney answered. "I *am* a minister!" he answered defiantly before once again realizing exactly who it was he was talking to.

"Then perhaps you should read the book again. Seems you read only the "Cliff Notes". Did you really think I took your side in all of those so called *Holy Wars?* The very phrase is a contradiction in terms."

Reverend Kinney suddenly realized that the voice was referring to his burning of the Koran. "But those people declared war on thousands of innocent people when they flew planes into the World Trade Center in New York and into the Pentagon here in Washington. They killed!"

"And you didn't," the voice answered. "Did you not feel that I would have felt that pain, their pain as well?" the voice continued. "There were Christians and Muslims in those towers. There were people of all faiths on those planes. Every child who grows up to become the soldier is one of mine, Christian, Muslim, Jew or Buddha. They all belong to me."

"But have you read the . . ."

"Koran . . . wrote it. Asian, African, Hindu religious texts . . . I wrote 'em all. Once again everyone reads what they want to read. You forget I am the God of Abraham *and* Isaac . . . and Jesus. Let me ask you this. Do you have children?"

Reverend Kinney pondered the weight of the question before answering. "I had children before I died." He said with the remorse of a father coming to grips that he would never see the faces of his children again.

"Technicality up here," the voice answered. "You still have children. Now which of your children do you love the most?"

"I love them all equally although John is a pain in the . . ."

"Ass?"

"Exactly! Wait a minute God doesn't cuss!"

"Not in heaven," the voice answered. "But you're not there yet. Like I said this is a holding room. The rules are different here. I get to let my hair down a little."

"So what do I do to get into heaven?" Suddenly Reverend Kinney dropped to his knees and began to pray, flailing on the ground and waving his arms wildly. "In the name of God our heavenly father I repent my sins . . . ."

"Stop it!" The voice commanded. "It's far too late for that. You were supposed to do that *before* you died . . ."

"I did . . ."

"You were supposed to mean it. I mean did you really think that burning those Korans is what *I* wanted? *Now* you have to do more."

"Like what?"

"You'll see . . . does the phrase "walk a mile in my shoes" mean anything to you?"

"Oh I get it . . . you want me to imagine I'm you," Reverend Kinney answered as if an angelic light bulb had just gone off inside his head.

"No I mean really walk a mile in my shoes! Or should I say his!"

Chapter fifteen

T he screen door wasn't much of a screen door at all and did more to permit entrance than prohibit the flies from coming in. As such the flies were more than willing to comply. It was framed in white paint that made its way onto the metal mesh in more places than one. The screen work was outlined in a type of cottage woodwork that hailed from a county far far away. It too was painted white accented by bent finishing nails that rusted with age. On the other side of the screen there was a hollow wooden door with three small windows strategically arranged in order of size. The largest was to the right and so they descended. Each was assigned its own separate color. It was trailer park sheik without the trailer park.

On the other side of the door there were screams.

They were the type of screams produced when one human violently attacks another.

"Go ahead and knock," the voice ordered Virgil Thompson, but Thompson was already frozen from fear. It was the type of fear produced following a horrible accident when one skids on the ice. Suddenly everything that once was became real again in an instant. Thompson knew all too well what was happening on the other side of the door. He had blocked it out of his mind but it was clear God had not.

"I don't think we need to do this," he answered.

"Remember, Virgil," the voice began. "This time *you* are not who you think you are." Glancing downward Thompson realized that for the first time in his death, he was no longer a white man, but instead black. "My best friend was . . ."

"Black," the voice said finishing the sentence. "I know. You laughed together and played together for days upon end. You once made a pact down by Big Wheeling Creek, that you would be friends forever. So what happened?'

"So you're saying I'm him knocking on the door asking me to come out?" he asked.

"No you're you, your thoughts at least. Just your body has changed. You already realize that something happened along the way to change the way you thought about people you once called friend . . ."

In that instance, a young Virgil Thompson came to the door. Thompson knew he was indeed looking back at his own past. The little boy was him.

Opening the door slowly at first and then squeezing through the tiny crevice of opportunity he had created. In his hand he held a small peanut butter sandwich and a half empty glass of milk. "Hurry," he said as if speaking directly to whoever was on the other side of the door and then closing the door behind him. "I don't want them to know I'm gone!"

"Why?" Thomson, now firmly entrenched in his new body asked instinctively. "I should at least come in and say hello to your folks . . ."

"Chores," his younger version answered. "I got a lot of work to do."

"I always did," the older Thompson answered softly under his breath as if a question had been asked, "I always did."

"What happened to the two of you?" the voice continued.

"We went our separate ways," Thompson answered.

"Did you?"

"I think we did. Stuff kinda happens. Before you know it you're in one place and he's in another. We just grew in opposite directions."

"I don't think it was quite that simple," the voice continued. "I think we need to take a little trip."

"Are we going to fly?" Thompson asked with the excitement of a little boy at Christmas time.

His mind raced back to the many TV shows he watched as a boy. His favorite was the "Hallmark Hall of Fame" series that flooded the airwaves during the holidays. He quickly remembered its version of a Christmas Carol by Dickens. In it George C. Scott went back as Ebenezer Scrooge to confront his past, his present and his future. Mostly he remembered the happy ending. Bu the thoughts of all of those encounters with ghosts still sent shivers down his spine. "So you will teleport me to my past?"

"No," the voice answered. "Not the teleport thing."

"Then how will we travel?"

"We're going to take the bus."

"The bus!"

"More appropriately," he continued. "Or as you so lovingly called it . . . the cheese."

Chapter sixteen

T hompson recognized the smell first.

It was a toxic mix of enamel paints that had long ago been banned and improperly mixed cleaning solvents already contaminated with the vomit of a child too nervous to attend classes. The hallways were lined with lockers, each bearing the graffiti of generations that had come and gone peering out from the paint that was supposed to hide it. Neon lights flicked overhead producing a strobe effect that provided for its own third world ambiance. Thompson knew he was back in grade school. Suddenly the door to room 213 opened. Thompson knew in an instance where he had been taken.

"Did I always sit in the back of the class?" he asked.

"If there were another row you would have sat there," the voice answered. "And seeing as how there weren't any other rows . . . yes you sat in the back of the class. I should also point out, most of the time you slept!"

Virgil Thompson surveyed the landscape of the classroom taking in the faces of the students who were seated. He quickly remembered his classmates who succeeded versus those who failed. He was in the back sleeping soundly. There sitting in the front row, hand raised prominently was his best friend growing up, Sylvester Wilson. "Show off!" he said sarcastically. "He had an answer for everything."

"That show off as you put it went onto receive a full scholarship to college. You on the other hand didn't finish high school."

"He was black!" Thompson replied. "It's all coming back to me now . . . seemed unfair. All the niggers got to go to college for free . . ."

"Be careful who you are calling nigger," the voice added. "You might want to look in the mirror."

"It's true, and let's be honest. No matter how many places you take me to in how many bodies, it ain't gonna change. The black people back then got everything. They got affirmative action and shit. They followed that man Martin Luther King to the grave and then the United States just rolled over on us white people. Once they started burning down all the cities white people got scared. They just gave up and gave them anything they wanted. They called it affirmative action . . . I call it the shaft. That's just the way it was and no matter how you look at it, it wasn't right."

"Is your world always that simple?" the voice asked. "Why is so hard for you to see life through the lens of another. You discounted hundreds of years of slavery . . ."

"There were white slaves too . . ."

"The numbers hardly compare. Blacks were enslaved, taken from their homeland, separated from their families and forced to survive. White slaves, as you call them came to this country as indentured servants. They were poor but they knew the length of their servitude. Yes times were rough but the playing field was hardly level."

"Everybody had it tough . . . we called it being poor back then."

"Then perhaps it's time you took another trip," the voice replied. "You have a lot to learn."

Chapter seventeen

T he first blow struck the face of the man whose body Peggy Wilson occupied.

At that precise moment she felt her lower lip split and, for the first time in her life, tasted blood. Almost instinctively she blocked the second punch with her left forearm and countered with a savage right cross striking her assailant squarely on the jaw, causing him to stagger backwards, regain his footing and take off running in the opposite direction. She was amazed at the strength the assault summoned. She was stunned by her anger. "What the hell?" she asked before being cut off in mid sentence.

"Was that?" the voice replied. "That was your neighbor and from the looks of things it doesn't seem that that much has changed since you were last here."

"*I* didn't live here," Peggy Wilson answered indignantly.

"You didn't but *he* did," the voice replied. "You forget . . . things are not as they seem. Have you already forgotten the erection?"

"Kinda hard to forget . . . excuse the pun," she answered. "I get it . . . I'm me, at least my mind is, but this is *his* body. But what does this have to do with heaven and hell?" she asked.

"One man's heaven . . . you see . . . is another man's hell," he replied. "This was your hometown. Consider it to be no different than your house. You walked past this neighborhood each and every day on your way to work and thought nothing of the people forced to live here. You had a choice to keep walking. They did not. It was as if you, and those like you, thought they deserved it . . ."

"We did mission work . . . just like you said."

". . . at Christmas time and Thanksgiving," the voice replied. Sadly for you . . . that right hook you dodged came in the heat of the summer when the violence in this neighborhood is always at its peak. Today it was a fist. Tomorrow it might a gun or a knife. Poor people need help all year round, not just when Christians feel the need to be . . . well *Christian*," the voice continued.

"But I sang in the choir and was a deaconess in my church," she answered defensively. "I wasn't perfect but I wasn't as bad as the others," she offered up by way of explanation.

"'And none of that means anything here," the voice began. "Do you think these people care about your white gloves during communion or the competition you won because your group of deacons stepped better than another group from another disenfranchised church?"

"I guess not . . ." she began to answer. She then began to wonder about the ritual of religion. She wondered aloud, "what would Jesus . . ."

"Do . . . what would Jesus do?" the voice answered finishing her sentence. "Taking up ones cross is not as easy as serving meals once or twice a year. It is about saving souls and going to those places where these souls needed to be saved. Sometimes those places are in our own back yards. So many people want to focus on problems overseas because exotic trips to foreign lands seem so romantic. But tell that the person who spent a lifetime inside the body you temporarily possess. As I said, this was his house and one of those rooms was filthy and yet you chose to walk past it each and every day."

"But he's a skinhead," she cried out, seeking anything in the way of mercy. "He spent his entire life preaching a philosophy of hate!"

"He's a child of God just like you," the voice answered. "Christ heeled lepers and walked among the tax collectors. He confronted the evils of his day without prejudice. If *I* turn my back on people like him, who else does he have? You see the skinhead, I see the child. Sometimes we learn the most from people by asking them the simplest of questions. In this case perhaps you should ask why he felt the need to shave his head."

"That's the way all them skinheads look," Peggy Wilson added. "They all shave their heads and walk around with mean expressions on their faces. They want to look like Nazi's."

"Each morning I listened as you mouthed the words to the 23rd Psalm. You talked about *"walking through the valley of the shadow of death"* but did little once there. You saw only what your fear allowed you to see. Your pace through this neighborhood was so fast that it would difficult to notice any detail. Not once did you ask if those shaven heads were meant to intimidate or *hide."* the voice said.

'What does he have to hide?" Peggy Wilson asked. "I mean look at me . . . him . . . his body is a walking billboard of pain," she continued.

"And that should be your first clue. The world would be a much better place if we only saw that which lie plainly in front of us. Follow me," the voice answered walking up the block until he came to a set of stairs in an abandoned house. With each step the layers of debris outside intensified until broken bottles crunched underfoot. The outside of the house had various layers of faded yellow crime tape. The steps on the front stoop were in disrepair, and a homeless man sat clutching a bottle of wine in a brown paper sack holding court on all who passed. A small yellow padlock barred entry from the outside. It mattered little. The homeless had pried open the plywood providing easy access through the window.

"Spare some change?" the homeless man asked. The stench of urine was overwhelming. The man looked as if he hadn't showered in weeks but yet also smelled of sweetness.

"You smell crack," the voice answered. "You didn't ask but remember I read your thoughts. It is like all things evil. Crack produces a pleasant aroma and smell and yet masks all the misery you see before you. You can see his condition but he cannot. Heroin addicts pull their teeth and scar. Self mutilation for the quick fix the drug provides," the voice said.

"You expect me to go in there?" Peggy Wilson asked.

"I expect you to open the door. That is all I have ever asked. In order to walk through the valley you first have to approach it. Look inside your right pocket, I think that's where you keep the key."

"Surely you're not saying that people live in this filth," she answered while groping for the key. He was right. As she reached down and pulled the key from her pocket, she was as much concerned with getting away from the people in the hallway as entering the door. Surely it couldn't be as bad on the inside as it was on the outside. She was wrong.

"This was your home for countless years," the voice said. "Your room is in the back."

Peggy Wilson could feel the heaviness in her footsteps. She glanced down at the thick black army boots where the sound originated. The body, his body, still seemed so foreign.

It seemed as if the weight of the entire world was in each step taken. She feared she was not far from the truth.

"I want you to pay particular attention to the photos on the small stand in the hallway," the voice explained.

Peggy Wilson continues down the hallway. The walls were scarred with the contents of shattered beer bottles that had been tossed their way. Various shades of paint hid feeble efforts to mask the misery inside the dwelling. Attempts to beautify were started and stopped in mid brush stroke. She noticed how the boards in the floor seemed to give way as she walked further. Even though she was not who she seemed, she did notice a certain familiarity with the settings, "Is this normal?" she asked. "I'm starting to feel a little like . . ."

"Him . . ."

"Yes . . . even though I think like me . . . I can almost hear his thoughts and feel his feelings as we go further. It's as if we are somehow . . ."

"One," the voice answered.

"Would you please stop . . ."

"Finishing your sentences?" the voice replied. "That would be impossible as I always know your every thought. Consider it an occupational hazard," the voice added.

As she made her way further down the hall she marveled at the fact that someone lived inside the building she passed almost daily on her way to church. As instructed, she stopped to examine the pictures on the small table. It wasn't much of a table but instead something that seemed to have been stolen from a hotel room in one of the shadier parts of town. Dust occupied the prominent position. The pictures hadn't been moved in years. Reaching down she picked one of the photos up. "He . . . I was a handsome young man," she said.

"Look closer," the voice added. "You have to look past the looks and look for the pain."

"I don't see anything that looks painful," Peggy began. "I assume that's me . . . and my mother . . . . but where's my . . ."

"Father? Those were my sentiments indeed," the voice answered. "Now take a closer look at the photo once more."

"My mother seems to be a rather attractive woman. She has such beautiful brown hair. Looks like she keeps it like I used too, pulled back in a bun." Her eyes then glanced at another photo on the stand. In that photo the hair was different. Carefully placing the first photo back in its dusty outline she reached down to pick up the other for closer examination. "Wait a minute," Peggy Wilson continued. "In this photo she seems to be wearing . . . and don't you dare finish my sentence this time . . . an afro!"

"And that would mean?"

"That would mean that she is . . . oh my God!"

"Black?"

"We'll you have your own classifications concerning things such as race, but yes she is, as you would call her, a black woman or African American or colored or Negro . . . or as you now prefer 'black'.

"But why does he . . . I . . . mean *me,* hate black people so much?"

"Take another look at that photo," the voice replied.

"Which one?"

"The one where you are smiling," he continued.

"Why would he keep all these photos?" she mused. She studied them more closely, in much the same manner she searched for missing clues in the back of those puzzles she loved in the Sunday supplement of the newspaper. There was always something hidden in plain sight. That's when she saw it . . . his hair. The little boy in the picture . . . his hair . . . It was . . . blond . . . and . . . .

Chapter eighteen

"Why would you bring me here?" Reverend Kinney asked. He recognized it as a restaurant that specialized in hot dogs that he had eaten at before in the past. There were the prerequisite photos on the wall. There was one of the owner with the mayor proudly cutting the ribbon. A rock star, whose fame had faded, once stumbled in. His picture was to the right of the mayor with the obligatory autograph underneath. The restaurant's first dollar was inside a frame that appeared to have been opened from time to time. And in the corner a small jukebox waited for a quarter to roar to life. "Are we going to get something to eat?"

"You'll see in just . . ." and then the voice turned and looked at his watch, ". . . three minutes to be exact."

"And what's going to happen then, I'll be visited by the Ghost of Christmas Past . . . as in Dickens?" Reverend Kinney continued sarcastically.

"Actually no . . . something far more real," the voice replied. "You might think more along the lines of . . . the ghost of bigotry present!"

Moments later the doors flew open and a group of high school boys poured in and sat at preselected booths. They were the Aryan equivalent of adolescent stupidity. Each appeared to be the perfect specimen of physical fitness, as was common for young men their ages. Each of them was wearing a varsity letter jacket proudly proclaiming that they had played some manner of high school sports. The large "W" indicated they played sports at nearby Wheeling High School. It was also symbolic of their race . . . white. It made things all so simple.

"I can see he does quite the business," Reverend Kinney began before being interrupted.

"Five . . . four . . . three . . . two . . . one . . ."

Without warning the group of teens leapt from where they had been seated and began shouting all manner of racist slurs. It was as if they had rehearsed their movements in the parking lot before entering the facility. Their spontaneity was meant to startle and they succeeded. A family of four seated in a nearby booth laid the cash equivalent of their check on the table and beat a hasty path toward the front door. Any innocence the youth once represented was gone in an instance.

"Go back to where you're from you towel head," one shouted.

"Camel Jockey!" another chimed in.

Sadly the verbal onslaught was just the beginning. The boys started smashing the glasses that just a short minute earlier had been filled with water on the adjacent table. The spill patterns foreshadowed what was to come. Their uncontrolled anger seemed to feed on each act and grew in its intensity. What at first appeared to be nothing more than a misguided teenaged prank, took a far more sinister turn, if one was possible?

"What are you doing?" One of the teens shouted, as if even he was caught by surprise at what was about to happen.

The sunlight caught the angle of the object perfectly and a small ray of light danced around the room in much the same manner as a light reflecting off a cheap disco ball. Across the room and headed toward Reverend Kinney was a young man brandishing a knife. He appeared to be no more than sixteen. The knife looked like it came from his mother's kitchen. He held it menacingly above his head.

Slowly he kept walking.

Reverend Kinney, still thinking he was inside his old body, began to speak out. "Young man I demand you put that down . . ."

"He can't see you," the voice stated.

"But I'm standing right in front of him," Reverend Kinney added with a matter-of-factness in his voice. "Of course he can see me. He'd have to be blind not to."

"No . . . he doesn't see *you!*" the voice added. In that moment, it seemed as if time slowed to a standstill. "You forget that *Reverend Kinney* is not here, only Suleiman Muhammad and that would be you!" he continued.

The knife was now in mid air and the teenager did not appear to be stopping. The anger, the rage on his face was undeniable. Still time seemed to be moving incredibly slow.

"What should I do?" Reverend Kinney asked. "If he stabs me will I feel the pain?"

"You will feel everything that *he* felt, and do everything that *he* did," the voice answered. "For all that is about to happen . . . you will be him."

As time once again sped up, almost reflexively, Reverend Kinney stepped to the side. The teen's forward momentum sent him crashing into a display case. Taking a moment to breathe, Reverend Kinney was about to celebrate his short victory over his assailant when he saw it. At first he hoped his eyes were playing tricks on him. Even though he was in the body of Suleiman Muhammad, the fear was palpable. He was not hurt but the teenager was. There was a large pool of blood forming underneath the teen near the broken display table and it seemed to be multiplying exponentially.

"Look what you did, Towel head," one of the teens shouted.

"I did?" Reverend Kinney replied.

"He had a knife!" Another screamed. "I saw it. He tried to kill Rodney, we all saw it!"

"But I did no such thing," Reverend Kinney answered. "He tried to kill me. He came at me with a knife. How will you explain all of this!" he added looking around at his trashed restaurant.

"How will you explain that?" another of the youths screamed pointing to their bleeding comrade in commotion who now was bleeding from the mouth as well.

In what seemed to be a matter of seconds the room was filled with the sounds of sirens and images of flashing lights.

"Thank God they're here!" Reverend Kinney declared. The sound of the approaching police signaled at least a temporary end to his hell. Still he gripped the large baseball bat that Muhammad kept behind the counter just in case.

"But they're not here for *you*," the voice answered.

"What do you mean?"

"You'll see."

"Freeze!" the first officer yelled as he burst through the door. "Down on the ground towel head!" he shouted. Then removing his pistol from its holster he screamed the command again. "I said drop the bat and down on the ground towel head!"

Reverend Kinney's eyes grew large as he first saw the bat in his hand and then the barrel of the pistol pointed at him that seemed without end. He promptly followed the officer's commands. Slowly placing the bat on the ground and then lowering his body into a position of surrender. In that very instant he felt the heel of a boot atop his neck. It was crushing the very oxygen from his lungs. "You have it all wrong!" he shouted struggling to get air.

"Another word from you and the coroner will have to sort this all out," the officer shot back. The boot pressed down further this time twisting slightly.

Reverend Kinney heard the sound of the trigger on the gun being cocked. The noise was deafening and sounded as if a cannon were being loaded. Once again, time seemed to be moving in slow motion. He could hear everything, every angry word, and they were all being directed at him. "But these young men assaulted me!" he screamed.

"We did not!" the ringleader of the teenagers responded. "We were here to get some hot dogs when he went all jJihad on us . . . shouting *Hello Akbar* or something in Arabic. When we tried to get out of the way he started throwing bottles of ketchup all over the place. He said he would make it look like we were vandalizing the place and that they would take his word over ours."

"But that's not the way it went . . . ." Reverend Kinney tried by way of explanation. His words fell upon deaf ears. The boot pressed down harder.

"I said shut your trap," the officer said applying more pressure to the boot. "How bad is the boy?" he asked.

"He'll live," the other officer responded. "Lucky for you . . . that's Jack Jones' kid. He owns the car dealership out on G.C. and P. road. You know . . . he's the City Councilman's kid!"

The boot that was applying pressure had accomplished its mission. Reverend Kinney inside Suleiman's body was starting to black out. "We'll let the judge sort it all out," he said clearly directing his attention to Muhammad. "In the meantime, you kids get the hell of here!"

Reverend Kinney faintly felt himself being led away in handcuffs and glanced to the side just enough to see the wounded teenager being loaded into the ambulance. He felt the pain from the incident, and the humiliation from what had happened. It was all so unfair. He wanted to protest but knew it would futile. He knew they could not see him, and wondered for the first time since arriving inside the holding room, just who *he* was. It was his first taste of the justice system as being someone other than white.

He hoped it would be his last.

What he didn't know was that the greatest judge of all was watching *his* every move.

Chapter nineteen

T he bus arrived on schedule belching black smoke from an engine that was badly in need of repair. It was green on the bottom and yellow on top. Rivets and layers of chipped enamel paint bore the markings of being inserted and removed multiple times especially near the engine housing. From the sound of the motor, one or more sparkplug failed to fire. The right door opened more slowly than the left and an elderly woman struggled to escape before both failed to completely.

"You'll have to ride in the *back* of the bus," the voice said softly with a discernible hint of sarcasm.

Virgil looked around him. The cars making their way up and down the streets seemed to be so old, and yet vaguely familiar. He estimated the time frame to be the late 50's or early 60's. The parking meters were old fashioned and the woman who walked up and down the sidewalks wore garments from a distant, long gone, age. Suddenly he remembered it all. It came back with the ferocity of a memory long ago tucked in the darkest recesses of a mind that spent years struggling to forget. He wanted the memory to stay there. It was a scene from his past.

"What the hell you looking at nigger!" an angry white man shouted from the other side of the street.

The response came quickly as Virgil studied his newfound body.

"That's right . . . I'm talking to you nigger boy," he again shouted much to the delight of the small mob of supporters that was gathered with him.

Virgil felt the hate rise up from within him. Slowly he felt his first clench and started across the street to retaliate before he felt the voice inside his head urge him to exercise caution.

"Don't forget who you are . . . now," the voice said. "You might find yourself on the wrong side of an angry mob.

It was at that precise moment that Virgil realized that the voice was more right than he wanted to believe. Glancing down at the black skin that glistened with sweat in the summer's sun, he knew he was no longer Virgil Thompson the Klan Grand Dragon standing on the opposite of the sidewalk. Instead, by some cruel twist of fate he had become his worst nightmare. He was black and unsure of how he appeared to the crowd assembled on the other side. For the first time in his life, or death, he was the 'nigger'. He felt the flare of his nostrils as he breathed in the atmosphere of hate. His pulse quickened at the same time his mind raced for an avenue of escape. He was sickened by the taste of bile rising through his stomach.

Was he Emmitt Till or worst, the target of the next lynch mob? Suddenly there was little time to sort it all out. Two words took away any time to reason.

"Get him!"

Thompson took off in the opposite direction, heading south on Main Street frantically trying to make contact with any sympathetic eye looking his way. None was found. With each stride he glanced backwards to see if the angry mob was still in pursuit. He felt his heart pound and chest heave as the angry mob grew closer and closer. He felt his own disbelief that such an attack would occur in broad daylight until he realized that he had once been on the other side of that street.

That's when it hit him.

The young man chasing him . . . was a younger version . . . of him! Worst still *he* was closing in. Suddenly Thompson knew exactly where he was. His mind had blocked out the incident because what was about to happen next was too horrible. In the instance between hanging onto life and accepting the fact that death was as inevitable as the nightmare he now found himself in, he stopped to face the angry mob just as the young man he had chased did so more than four decades earlier. And just as was the case then, the first blow . . . came from a younger version of him. Virgil Thompson, inside the body of a black man was being attacked by a younger version of himself. He could see the rage, and soon he would feel the anger.

The punches seemed without end. He tried to fight back but he was vastly outnumbered. Any attempt to block a punch coming from the left, left open the door to a blow coming from the right. He heard the sound of a front tooth shattering. He could taste the saltiness of his own blood. The pain coming from his groin caused him to double over and curl up in the fetal position in an attempt to ward off as much pain as possible . . . the punches . . . . the kicking. For the first time since he had died, he felt as if he were to die again.

"Have you seen enough," the voice inside his head said softly.

"Yes," Virgil cried out as the angry mob unleashed their anger upon him.

But their voices grew silent. The next voice he heard was the one that would render the ultimate judgment.

"I don't think you have suffered enough," the voice said. "There is more . . . much much more!"

Chapter twenty

"His hair is blond!" Peggy Wilson said softly as she picked up the photo and examined it more closely. "But his mother is black," she continued. Placing the photo back atop the small table she turned and asked, "What does it mean?"

"It means just what it seems to mean," the voice answered by way of riddled explanation. "It means that the human existence is an ever unfolding mosaic of sometimes joy and sometimes pain and sometimes confusion. In this case it is all of the above. You have before you an innocent child, born of a union that was not of his doing and yet he bore the scars of that union his entire life. He was, if you will, trapped between two races."

"But that doesn't explain the anger," Peggy Wilson explained. "There are lots of children born of interracial parents. They don't grow up to be skinheads," she continued.

"No . . . that fact alone does not. But your thoughts are based on things as they are now. Back then things were much different. As is the case with all things, that which appears on the surface only hides the pain that bubbles from beneath. Sometimes all we need to do to uncover that truth is to wait. His father will be coming by any minute," the voice said. "It will explain a lot."

As the door opened, the woman in the picture emerged arm and arm with a man Peggy Wilson found to be vaguely familiar. She was the woman in the photo, but he . . . he . . . was a former classmate. Someone she thought she knew. It was a man she once called her friend.

The man violently threw the woman to what was once a sofa, ripping off her blouse and what remained of soiled panties. Unzipping his trousers at the same time, he pulled the belt from his pants and began to strike her across the face making sure the buckle made contact with each blow. His anger seemed to be directed toward her face. "Admit it you little slut!" he shouted angrily. "You enjoy it!"

As Peggy Wilson watched, she noticed a small boy quivering in the corner. It was the little boy in the photo, the boy with the curly blond hair. He was being forced to watch it all. He was forced to watch the man brutally assaulting his mother. He was powerless to do anything about it. He was crying. The violent sexual assault continued until Peggy could take no more. "Make him stop," she cried out!

"I cannot stop that which has already occurred," the voice explained. "Nor can you expect a son to take up arms against either his *father* or his *mother*," he continued.

Then it happened. Peggy Wilson realized she was beginning to feel the pain . . . his pain. With each blow that landed, she winced. Her body recoiled at the sexual assault that followed. She wanted to vomit. She wanted to do something but she couldn't. She was frozen. She was as motionless as the little boy in the corner. She was *him*. She wanted to kill the man who was striking her mother, she wanted to kill her mother for allowing him to do so. What happened next made her want to kill herself.

"Now take your money and go get high you lousy slut," he said throwing a wadded up pile of crumpled dollar bills her way.

She hurriedly picked up the money first and then assembled what was left of her clothes next. That's when she noticed the young boy cowering in the corner. "What are you looking at you little tramp," she screamed. "Now get the hell out of here. Go play or do something you worthless piece of shit!"

"In the absence of love," the voice said to Peggy, "people often chose fear or power. Hate is the devil's strongest tool. There is so much about this young boy you don't know . . ."

"I don't believe I want to know any more," she said softly between sobs.

"Oh but you do," the voice added. "You want to know more, because this little boy holds the key to *your* salvation!"

Chapter twenty-one

Reverend Kinney awoke in the jail cell as Suleiman Muhammad wondering why he had received no medical attention for the severe beating he suffered at the hands of police in the "holding area." His eyes were puffy and jaw seemed to be swollen shut. The lip that was split early on in the assault was now a swollen mess. He wanted to speak but the words would not come. Reflexively his tongue searched his mouth for what once was a tooth. It was gone. Everything was all too painful.

He could see, but barely and he could hear. He could only smell and the jail cell smelled of hate. To his surprise, the police in the room weren't paying any attention to him at all. Instead all eyes were fixed on the TV.

"We now interrupt your regular scheduled programming to bring you a special report," the announcer intoned. The *"Breaking News"* graphic that he could faintly make out seemed to indicate that something was indeed either happening

or about to happen. The camera in the studio then shifted to a reporter in the field.

"I'll be dammed. He's going to do it," one of the officers remarked. "I never thought the son of a bitch would go through with it," he added.

"All hell is going to break lose if he does," another replied. "I didn't think he had the nerve," he continued.

The reporter in the field picked up the drama. "Despite warnings from the White House and the Secretary of Defense, the Reverend Eugene Kinney has decided to go ahead and burn 150 copies of the Koran, the Muslim Holy Book, which he says were donated by others who share his extreme religious beliefs."

"How do you like that towel head?" one of the cops asked, ridiculing Muhammad. "Where are your seventy two virgins now?" he continued.

Then, striking a match and holding it high in the air, Reverend Kinney set fire to the pile of Korans. At first, it appeared as if they refused to burn, then slowly the first caught fire, followed by a second and then flames roared into the sky. As the images of the burning Korans filled the screen, images of angry mobs protesting the move occupied a smaller box in the upper right hand corner. They were scenes pouring in from places like Cairo Egypt, and in Paris where there were considerable Muslim populations. In the center of it all, Reverend Kinney and two of his most ardent supporters grinning from ear to ear like a Cheshire cat in some children's novel. He had achieved his fifteen minutes of fame, but at what cost?

"Reverend Kinney?" a reporter asked. "Now that you've done what you promised, was all this necessary?"

"Someone had to send a message that we Christians won't take being led to the slaughter like an innocent flock of sheep," Reverend Kinney answered. "It wasn't me, but the Lord who lit that match," he continued. "It was a Christian God who set fire to these Korans!"

"Interesting choice of words," the voice said softly.

"You're here," Reverend Kinney said, still nursing the wounds in the body of Suleiman Muhammad.

"I never left," the voice replied. "I am with you now, just as I was in that jail cell with the man whose body you now occupy."

"Then you can make it all stop," Reverend Kinney pleaded.

"I cannot change the past," the voice replied. "But *you* could have stopped it all. You had a choice. You could have led your flock that day to stop the injustice that occurred in the shop of Suleiman Muhammad, but that wouldn't have attracted the attention of the world's media. Because of the choices you made, all choice have been taken away from everyone involved. You unleashed hate upon this tiny community and all that goes it. Now, because of you, hate will have its reign."

"But you are God!" Reverend Kinney screamed out, wondering why the police in the room did not hear him.

"And you are man," he answered. "*Now* you chose to know me. Where was your familiarity with my work when you were burning those Korans? Did you think that doing so would please me?"

"But they had to be stopped!" he snapped in response. "They killed thousands on September 11th. They were going to kill us all," he continued.

"No . . . hate killed thousands that day . . . just as it will claim countless lives on this day and countless more in the days to follow. Will you claim credit for the suicide bomber who targets Americans overseas because of what *you* did? You simply chose to see the hate that is not of your own hand. Do you care about the little boy who suffers at the boot of a soldier overseas who mocks him the same way you mock Muslims across the world? Did you care about the life of a small hot dog vendor that you affected simply by burning *his* holy book?"

"But his religion is an affront to what you taught us in the bible . . ."

"Careful clergy . . . I am the father of Abraham *and* Isaac. Did you not think that I was capable to defending myself? Did you not believe that the God who created and once destroyed the world could handle something as simple as hate? No . . . it is you who are an affront to what you have been taught. You, who stood in the pulpit and preached hate in my name. This man . . . this body you now occupy was innocent. He simply wanted a better life for his family. What man, no matter his religion, wants less? You were not there with him, for your celebration brought with it, *his* darkest hour.

"I do not understand . . ."

"What is to happen next will be of your doing not mine," the voice said.

Suddenly the door to the jail cell began to open.

"Like *him*,' the voice continued, "you will feel everything. This is what hate begets!"

Chapter twenty-two

T here were three men standing on the corner. Each wore the prerequisite jeans and white tee shirt, with a small pack of cigarettes rolled up in the sleeve of a muscled and crudely tattooed arm. Each had sunglasses that originated from the local five and dime, and each was white. They stood in front of "Doc's" a small drug store that doubled as a place where sodas were sold to cool off. On most days "Doc's" welcomed all who fit through his door and were willing to pay. Today was different. Today all traffic passed to the other side.

"Oh God," Virgil cried out. Even though it had been decades, the events that were about to unfold would define him for the rest of his life, and into his death. "Please Stop! I know what is going to happen," he said. "This day has haunted me every day of my life."

"But not once did you do anything to make amends," the voice explained.

As they spoke, a pickup truck pulled up. The truck was old. The tailgate, which was a different color than the rest of the truck, made the truck appear to be a hybrid between a Chevy and a Ford. The truck backfired, as it came to rest, creating even more tension. The young man on the other side of the road was no more than fifteen, sixteen at best. His face appeared as if never graced by a razor, and a small amount of peach fuzz grew over his upper lip.

"Roger's car broke down!" One of the men on the corner shouted. "We need your help!"

"What's wrong with your truck?" The boy yelled back. It was clear from his actions, he knew trouble was brewing and wanted no parts of it.

"Everybody knows it broke down," the man answered curtly as if in no mood to accept back talk from one so young. "This thing won't make it. Besides . . . even if we could get it runnin' for long . . . it's almost out of gas! So hurry up kid and get your daddy's keys."

The young man surveyed the group making their way across the street. They were his father's best friends. They were men he knew for years. They were older and white and mean. He knew they were men who would have to be reckoned with. He had also heard the rumors of what was to happen. He had hoped they wouldn't do what had been talked about. He had to talk to "Doc." Doc was the only person he trusted. "I need to talk to Doc first," he replied hoping to stall for time.

"Doc can wait," the oldest of the men shot back. "What we getting' ready to do will make history . . . now is you in or out?"

The boy paused for what seemed to be an eternity before looking up, as if asking God for assistance. When none came he answered, "I suppose pa won't mind."

The die was cast.

A few seconds later, his father's truck was filled with the men who once stood on the corner. As he looked back in the rearview mirror as they sped out of town, he saw Doc standing inside the doorway looking out.

"All you had to do was say no," Virgil mouthed as the events unfolded before him. "You should have been tougher kid," he added. "For all of us . . ."

A short time later the truck belonging to the boy's father was filled with an even larger mob of angry men toting shotguns and headed up Main Street. The housing projects were on the right hand side of the road, and, as they approached a young black man walking in the opposite direction, the boy instinctively applied the brakes. He had seen it all before, but this time was different.

"Ain't got time for that now," the man in charge said hastily. "Got bigger plans today," he said with an eerie smirk across his face. "Much bigger . . . head north toward Macedonia Baptist Church. That's where all them niggers go to pray."

It was Saturday. Macedonia, as always on the second Saturday in July, was holding its annual church picnic. The men of the congregation spent the morning setting up the tents and getting the grills for the barbecue ready. The women spent their mornings in the kitchen preparing the pies and other staples that made the picnic famous. Each family had its own recipes and each bragged it was the best. The children did not discriminate. They eagerly awaited the highlight of the picnic, a watermelon eating contest in which there were no losers, just happy seed spitting kids. As it was already two in the afternoon the main meals had already been consumed and everyone was gathered around four large steal tubs where the watermelons were kept cool.

"We took em' the ice just this morning," the man in the passenger seat explained. "Wait till they get a load of this year's watermelon eating contest," he added gleefully. "Ain't no better way to take care of a bunch of niggers than with their own watermelons."

"Yeah . . . wait till they find out that these ain't no ordinary watermelons," another man in the truck added with the slightest of southern drawls. "Let's just say some of em gonna pack a punch!"

Unknown to the men of Macedonia, two of the watermelons were hollowed out and loaded with nails and blasting powder. The timer in the small clock inside was set for exactly 2:15. The two dummy watermelons were placed beside a much larger pile of melons to be consumed, along with the others, as part of the contest. The ticking of the clock was hidden by the sounds of the celebration and murmurs of cheering children. Hundreds were gathered near the pile, with dozens of kids lined up to participate. They didn't stand a chance.

"Please," Virgil pleaded. "I don't want to watch!" he added.

"You forget you are no longer Virgil Thompson," the voice replied. "In fact you are no longer a white man in the back of a pickup truck. You are there," he said pointing to a young man in the third row of the water melon eating contest.

"But I thought I was only to travel backwards in bodies inside the holding room?" he protested.

"It would be safe to say that the tables have been turned!" the voice answered.

"That's me?" he questioned. Then his mind raced through the flood of headlines that blast produced. Thompson remembered the arrests, the trial and finally, when all interest had waned, the release of the last victim from the hospital after years of rehab therapy. "I know who that is," he said. "He was gravely wounded in the blast and never walked again. I am walking and talking. That couldn't be me!"

"No," the voice replied. "That is not you."

Relief replaced the fear that just ago consumed Thompson's every thought. Moments later it returned. "If that is not me . . . then which one am I.?"

"I was pointing to the woman standing *behind* him. As is always the case, it is the collateral damage that is forgotten long after the event. In this case, it is a woman who is pregnant with child and she has chosen today to tell her husband the joyous news."

Virgil wanted to move. He wanted to run toward the picnic and warn all who had gathered. He wanted to shout, but his legs would not move and his voice made no sounds. He was powerless to do anything, except to watch. Seconds became an eternity as Thompson noticed the secondhand on the clock in the church steeple. 2:14 had passed and the second hand was sweeping toward 2:15. It was only a matter of seconds.

Tick . . . tick . . . tick . . .

Suddenly the air was filled with the force of multiple explosions sending the near lifeless bodies of young children flying through the air and the people in the crowd fleeing in panic. What was once a celebration would soon be a crime scene, with dozens of victims and body parts strewn for hundreds of yards to be collected by evidence technicians.

Then there was the screaming . . . the sound of children crying out for their parents . . . the sound of parents frantically searching for their loved ones . . . the sound of dying.

"Make it stop!"

But the voice was silent.

The smaller children closest to the water melons died instantly creating a sea red seeds and flesh and blood. Many of the spectators were gravely wounded. Those who escaped immediate harm were psychologically scarred for life by what they witnessed next.

Virgil Thompson saw it too. Slowly the cloud created by the explosion started to life. All eyes were now on the truck on the opposite side of the street. The people in the crowd saw it. Virgil Thompson focused on one man in particular . . . . himself, laughing. He also saw the others shooting the walking wounded as they fled for cover.

He wondered why.

Chapter twenty-three

"D o you know where you are?" The voice asked.

The room was dark, but had a familiar smell. It wasn't the smell of a roast cooking or a pie baking in the oven, but, instead the smell of sin. It was the familiar smell of all things horrible that happen in life, but cannot be erased by memory no matter how hard we try. It was the smell of things, tastes, which come back in the moments before or after an auto accident, or sudden brush with death. Dylan Walsh recognized it almost instantaneously.

"And why are we here?" he asked angrily.

"I thought it better to ask *you*," the voice replied. "After all, it is *your* life that we are looking at." As he spoke, the colors on one of Walsh's tattoos seemed to come to life as if responding to the vary incident itself. The letters rose from the flesh and danced just above the surface of the skin. It burned. "I see you can't control your thoughts as well as you might like," he said pointing out the obvious.

"Maybe I just don't want to revisit this particular part of my life," Walsh replied. "Didn't nothing good happen here, ain't nothing good gonna come from it," he continued.

"Then why the anger?" The voice asked.

"I believe you know the answer to that question already," Walsh answered. "That's why we're here, isn't it?"

As he spoke the darkness of the room was illuminated by the opening of a door. At first it was a crack allowing the light on the other side to spill into the room. There standing inside the doorway stood the towering silhouette of a man. The silence was shattered by the sound of his footsteps. He entered slowly, whispering in quiet tones, so as not to awaken those on the other side of the door.

"Shhhh," the man said.

Almost reflexively Dylan Walsh huddled in the corner of the room. "Don't come near me," he cried in the muffled sounds of a little boy protesting against the wind. "I'll hurt you," he added. "I can you know."

"Now now . . ." the man said softly placing his finger aside his lips to once again signal his need for silence. "This won't hurt at all now will it? Has it ever?" he answered.

Dylan Walsh said nothing; instead he continued cowering in the corner. He knew what was going to happen next. Every muscle in his body and every nerve tensed. He began to shake violently. He could feel it. He could smell it. Slowly his jaws began to clamp shut.

As the door closed behind him, the man started to make his way toward the little boy cowering in the corner. He began removing his clothing with each step he took, until six steps into the room he was completely naked and pulling back the sheets on the little boy's bed. Motioning for the boy to join him he said, "Lay down beside me." There was a menacing tone in his voice that, while not threatening in volume, was certainly threatening in its intent.

As the man watched, Dylan walked over removing his own clothes in the process. Then standing beside the man, he too lifted up the sheets and slid his own nude body next to the man. And then it began. "Please . . ." the little boy moaned in protest.

"Make it stop!" Dylan begged.

"It has already happened," the voice explained. "I cannot change that which has already occurred, only that which is yet to come . . . ."

"Then why did you bring me here?" Dylan cried out. "That man raped me over and over and over again. It happened on this night, and the night after, and every night that followed until I . . ."

"Slit his throat?" the voice answered. There was a deadly pause. "You waited until you were old enough, strong enough, and then you answered the call of hate with violence."

"Exactly . . . the sick bastard had it coming to him. I cut him good and don't regret a single moment of what I did. Not one blessed minute!"

"He was your stepfather," the voice explained.

"He was a criminal . . . a sex offender . . . . a rapist . . ."

"So be it . . . . but we are not here for him," the voice explained. "His soul was lost long before he entered your bedroom. *Your* soul is at stake now. We are here for you." As he spoke Dylan Walsh felt his body levitating. The door to the room was open once more, revealing the little boy and the man in bed together. The man was sleep, but the body of the little boy heaved up and down, to signal sobbing. But this time, Dylan Walsh was not inside that body, but instead over it. The pain, the fear that had gripped him just seconds ago had faded. The hate that he felt rising up in his body was gone but as they floated down the hallway he knew it was soon to return. "Why are we going here?" he asked.

"Because this is the answer you long have wanted to know . . ."

"What answer would that be? Like I said, I slit the old bastard from head to toe. I got even for what happened all those years . . . case closed . . . over! Just send me straight to hell!"

"Judgment is never quite that simple," the voice replied.

Slowly the door to the next room down the hall began to open. Dylan knew exactly where it led. It was his mother's bedroom. He had always wondered whether she knew what had happened or why he chose to kill the man she wed. He half expected to see her asleep, not knowing what was happening next door. He prayed that would be the case. His real fears were quickly realized.

She was wide awake.

She was crying.

"She knew?" he asked. "All along she knew and did nothing?" he continued.

"She knew," the voice explained. "But it would not be safe to say that she did nothing. She did plenty.

Chapter twenty-four

"Where are we now?" a startled Reverend Kinney asked. He once again surveyed his body. The wounds from the savage police beating had healed. Gone were the gash on his lip, and the welts on his back. The bones that were broken during the savage attack had healed as well. He was curious to understand why. "What happened to the police?"

"The beating has not yet occurred," the voice commanded. "You are no longer the man you tormented but once again yourself. Do you recognize this day?"

Reverend Kinney thought as he surveyed his surroundings. It was sunny outside. A breeze blew the freshly pressed dresses of the women as they crossed a large parking lot, lined with small saplings that appeared to be newly planted. Each line in the lot was freshly painted. Everything about the place was new. What was not new was young. In an instant he knew exactly where he was standing. He was standing in the parking lot of a large mega church located in the suburbs . . . a church that frequently made headlines for feeding the hungry and clothing the sick. Sadly he knew that sort place all too well. "Did you bring me here to torment me further?" he asked. "This can't be worse than the police beating or that savage attack inside the store!" he blurted out.

"Those were the experiences you caused," the voice replied. "Surely by now you must be wondering why you acted the way you did. Or do you believe that you were just born this evil man who paraded around as a man of God?"

Reverend Kinney was angered by the comments and perplexed. Based on his own calculations he knew he had already died and either had gone or was going to hell. All he needed now was to reverse course . . . a course correction. Why was God judging him now? He had seen the error of his ways and was ready to pay for his sins. There was nothing left to learn. He would repent and go to heaven with the rest of the sinners he preached about weekly. He would claim Jesus Christ as his Lord and savior and automatically the gates of heaven would open up with welcoming arms.

God, of course, was a God of forgiveness. What was left?

"Oh I get it," he began, smiling from ear to ear. "You want to show me what happens to a man who faithfully follows God's commands," he continued. "I get it, if I had stayed the course this would have been my reward! I would have had a mega church like that one."

"And that is where you are wrong," the voice replied. "Doing God's work is no guarantee of heaven on earth. It only means that when you get to heaven you won't have to worry about your judgment. Unlike you, there are people who enter into heaven without having to repent for a life of sin. They live their lives according to my word and when they die theirs is a natural place in heaven. Some live lives of wealth, others swear a vow of poverty while others still part with all of their worldly possessions to take up the cross . . . to each his or her own reward."

"I did that," Reverend Kinney answered defensively. "I built that church from a small storefront. There was nothing there when we moved in but old furniture and rats. It took a whole week just to cart out the junk. We spent countless hours removing dirt and painting walls that had never before been painted. Once I opened my doors I took in the sick and baptized the entire congregation!"

"It is not *what* you did," the voice began by way of explanation. "It is *why* you did it that has caused your soul to be in jeopardy."

"In jeopardy? I did it to serve you . . ."

"You did not," the voice interrupted sternly with deeper bass tone. "It is written you cannot serve me and the ways of man too and yet that is what you tried to do. Your interests weren't in your salvation but instead your bank account. There you are sitting in the third row from the front."

"I'm in church . . . so what?"

"When I sent my Son to earth, it was the church that caused him the greatest agony. He could accept the shortcomings of man but to use the church as a place of making money was one of the greatest sins of all. That is why he overturned the tables of the money changers inside the temple. You weren't just in a church; you were in a wealthy church and that is all that you saw. You failed to see the good that they did there in my name. You could only see the pews full of people. Look at you as the collection is being taken. I could almost see you counting the dollars and wondering how long it would take you to reach that level of success. You didn't burn the Koran because you thought it to be the work of sinners. You burned the Koran for publicity to bring more people into your church. You reasoned more parishioners would mean more money. You bastardized my name in the name of hate and greed!"

"Is it a sin to want to be successful in all that you do?"

"You dare to question my judgment? Your actions from that day forth were guided by jealously and greed. You forget that I not only hear what is in your prayers but what is in your heart. In your heart of hearts you wanted what all other preachers who take up my name in vain want, you wanted money! You wanted to use the church as a means to wealth. That makes you no different than the crack dealers on the corner who seek to profit off of the pain of others."

"But with that money I could feed the hungry . . . ."

"Silence!" The voice commanded angrily in a tone that seemed to cause the very foundation of the earth to shake. "You shall sin no more!"

And then there was only darkness.

Chapter twenty-five

T he sound of the explosion was deafening, and for a moment anything and everything around him seemed to be moving in slow motion. The tables at a nearby coffee shop shook violently and the patrons spilled into the streets. For that brief moment it seemed as if the gates of hell themselves had opened up. A huge cloud arose from the area where the explosion occurred. The wounded emerged one by one, dazed and confused and bloodied from the attack. Sadly they were the lucky ones.

"Suleiman! Suleiman! Are you okay?" The little boy asked excitingly, drawing deep breaths each time he uttered the name of his friend.

Muhammad immediately began to check his body for signs of damage before realizing that the wounds he would suffer would never heal. But in that instance he was half a world away in another time and place. "Where is Ahmed?" he screamed. "Ahmed!" His eyes darting wildly back and forth, he started to run away, then stopped, and started running in the opposite direction. "Ahmed!" he screamed again and again, and again, until his voice started to grow hoarse, "Ahmed!"

Ahmed had been playing with a soccer ball just down the road in the moments just before the explosion. He was close enough to be seen but too far to get to before the blast. Now he was nowhere to be found. Instead the area where he once stood had been eviscerated. Smoke rose from the crater the bomb created. A small tree that once provided shade for endless childhood stories was now a splintered stump. The small powder blue car that was parked alongside the road for days upon end was no more.

There was nothing.

There was no sign of Ahmed.

"It was the car," he thought as he watched the others silently search for their loved ones. "Ahmed was playing near the car!" His mind raced backwards in slow motion assembling each and every minute and then the seconds before the blast. The truth was, there hadn't been a day that he hadn't done so. He remembered the sound returning to his ears. He remembered his own screaming as it intensified. "Ahmed!" he cried out. "Ahmed!" But there was no Ahmed to be found. He knew instantly his best friend in life, his only brother, was dead.

"Why did you bring me here?" he asked painfully, an air of pleading in his voice.

"Because is it part of who you are," the voice replied. "We are the sum of all of life's experiences . . . the good and the bad."

Muhammad surveyed the landscaped. Everything was so real. The bomb was real, the sound of the explosion, the explosion itself. He could even smell the nitrates that authorities would later determine were used to provide the explosive power. Thirteen people died that day, but the other twelve mattered little . . . only the one. Ahmed, his brother, was dead.

"I did not seek revenge," he said. "Too long we have lived with an eye for an eye. Even though I lost my brother, I knew it was time for the killing to stop."

"And for years I watched," the voice answered.

Still the pain of reliving the worst moment of his life caused Muhammad to want to vomit. "When my parents saw the opportunity for us to come to America they seized it. We never looked back . . ."

"Not even for a moment?" the voice asked. "Both you and I know better than that. Admit it, when Reverend Kinney burned the Koran, you wanted to seek revenge. It wasn't about the Koran now was it?"

Suleiman searched his heart as the words began to set in.

"It was about your brother. Upon being released from the hospital you wanted revenge. You planned to kill a man for reasons he would never know. If not, why didn't you seek out the young men who beat you . . . or the cops that did the same? Did you not once think about the consequences of your actions?" the voice asked.

"What do you mean?" Muhammad asked. "I would have simply rid the world of yet another bigot. Rev. Kinney knew the fuse he was lighting before he lit it. You know of the humiliation I suffered in that town simply because of my religion. They called me towel head, and camel jockey. They spit on my food and sent it back saying I did so. They beat me to within an inch of my life! How much must a man suffer before even you say it is too much?" he asked.

"If I remember correctly the answer is 40 times 40," the voice answered. "There is never a time for hate to be answered with hate. That is how the cycle begins and the ending is always the same. One man takes another man's mule so they fight. That fight leads to a larger fight involving other members of the families and the feud continues for so long, that no one remembers the mule or why it started. Wars are fought *by* poor people *for* rich people. Terrorism begets even more terrorism . . ."

"But I stopped," Muhammad reasoned. "Just moments before I was to detonate the bomb, I stopped!"

"I know that," the voice answered, "but the rest of the world does not. As far as they are concerned, another terrorist was taken out just before he was to detonate a bomb that would have killed dozens. Your actions would be no different in history than the actions that took the life of your brother . . ."

"But in your Bible it is written that we are justified to take an eye for an eye . . ."

"That was in the Old testament!" The voice responded. "You read the Old Testament and embraced it for your own selfish reasons. Mankind became too violent. I gave man the power of the atom and he built a bomb. I gave him free speech and he created hate speech. Did you ever wonder why the man responsible for the Nobel Peace Prize, Alfred Nobel, was also the man who invented ballistite and dynamite? He saw that the fruits of his genius became his potential legacy and decided to change. I gave you great men of peace and you gunned them down in the name of hate. Need I continue?"

"But he burned the Koran!"

"He burned paper. All religious books are paper. It is the *men* who use hate to continue the cycle of violence. They determine the act of destruction is more than that. Think about it? Would any God be threatened by the simple burning of a book? You place us on pedestals and then remove us from those pedestals at your will. What you were prepared to do that day was no different than what those men did to your brother. You were acting out of ignorance and hate."

Slowly the dust settled on the street before him and yet this time something was diffcrent. It was as if everything was moving in reverse. The tree that provided the shade was there, as was the powder blue car that had been parked there and abandoned for weeks. And there was Ahmed . . . his little brother . . . smiling, playing soccer just as he left him. Muhammad couldn't believe his eyes. His little brother was alive again. "Thank you," he mouthed in appreciation. As he looked up he saw his brother motion for him to join the game

"He sees you as you were," the voice answered. "He is in heaven. He cannot see hate. He only sees love and back then you were filled with it. He wouldn't recognize your present form."

"Will I be able to join him?"

"That depends upon you."

Chapter twenty-six

"I don't recognize any of this," Virgil Thompson explained as the horrors of what he had done at the church picnic began to set in. Occasionally his body would still shiver as he recounted what he had seen, and prior to that, lived through. "What could *this* possibly have to do with what I have done?" he asked. "Now I know I don't deserve to go to heaven. Ain't no need fighting it, so just send me straight to hell," he added. "I'll fit in fine with all the people like me who are already there. Hell, I'll probably see some people I know," he added trying to add humor to a moment where there was none to be had.

"If only it were that simple," the voice explained. "But they arc not. Remorse is typical when we are confronted with the sins of our lives. None of us is without sin," he added. "You are no different . . . only the levels of sin vary from person to person . . . but make no mistake about it, none is without sin."

Virgil sensed calm for the first time in what seemed to be an eternity. The setting before him was as far away from hell as humanly possible. Leaves fell from the trees at the slightest of winds in the brightest of colors. Blue skies welcomed the crisp air of autumn. Still, the moment that was presented was as foreign as the countries he had seen on the covers of brochures. Countries he grew up knowing he would never visit. This sight, too, was as far away as those faraway places. He was looking at a funeral for someone people admired.

As Thompson watched, a group of soldiers folded a flag neatly and with precision. It was as if they had done it over and over again, when in fact they had. The men stood straight and ridged before one of the soldiers approached a small boy and presented the flag to him. The boy, who appeared to be no more than three or four, offered a small salute and accepted the flag. Then returning to the statuary men, he listened intently to another man barking orders. The voice was firm, but not loud enough to disturb the solemnity of the occasion. In unison the seven soldiers pointed their rifles toward the sky in a solitary line, and fired.

"Fire!" The men reloaded. The little boy winced. "Fire!" A second reload. Fire!" And then the guns fell silently to their sides. In perfect military formation they marched off to the side and stopped again.

Three volleys of seven were discharged from the guns. It was a twenty one gun salute. When it was over, only the slightest wisp of gunpowder could be seen in the air. The service in all its pomp and circumstance was over. The soldiers were marching off to another funeral, another twenty one gun salute.

"That boy is you," the voice said softly.

Thompson couldn't believe what he was seeing. How was it possible that such a significant episode in his life had been blocked out? Was it possible to forget a funeral? It was all starting to come back to him . . . the cemetery, the flag. It was his father . . . . the funeral of his father. "That was my *father's* funeral," he said as the torrent of repressed memories began to return flooding his conscious with guilt as he tried to process what he had just seen and somehow forgotten. "How old was I? How did I . . . ."

"You were three years old," the voice replied. "You were but a child."

As they stood and watched the casket being lowered into the ground more memories returned. A woman seemed to wait for the others to leave, before walking up and allowing a single white rose to fall innocently onto the pine wood box as it was being lowered. "That's when it happened," he said. "It started to rain. From then on it rained hard for more than week. I've hated the rain ever since," he said softly.

"And from that day forward I watched as you cowered in each and every thunderstorm that came your way," the voice answered. "So many of our fears are shaped when we are so very young, and yet so few of us understand why," he added. "That is why I watch over the children so carefully. You were one of those children. I watched over you that day."

"But what does that have to do with how I turned out?" Virgil asked. "My father died when I was young. So what! It happened to a lot of kids back then, World War II, Korea, Vietnam and such. Being afraid of the dark is one thing, but killing a man is another. Right is right and wrong is wrong and I done wrong . . . plain and simple," he added.

"Nothing is either *plain,* or *simple*," the voice added. "Watch!"

As the various members of the family were making their way back to their respective cars, Virgil Watched as T.L. Gray Sr. approached his grandfather.

"He's been burying people as long as I can remember," Thompson said. "Don't seem like he ever died!"

"He did," the voice answered. "His son picked up the slack."

"It was a lovely ceremony wasn't it?" T.L. Gray remarked.

"Why yes," Virgil's Grandfather answered. "How can I thank you?" he asked.

"Now is not the time for these matters," Gray answered. "I would rather discuss it in the privacy of your home," he added. "You son left several bills unpaid . . . large bills. Preparing his body was not *easy* due to the severity of the wounds he suffered," Gray continued. "In fact preparing your son's body for what you've just seen required more work than I anticipated . . ."

"I thought the military handled all of that?" Virgil's Grandfather asked.

"They did but your wife asked me to take matters into my own hands when questions were raised about the *quality* of the care your son would receive," he replied.

"They were your questions!" Virgil's Grandfather answered curtly not wanting to let on that something was wrong at a funeral of all places. "*You* were the one raising questions about how well the military would care for our son. *You* planted those seeds of doubt!"

"The past is the past," Gray answered. "We must deal with the matters at hand, and those matters include the bill for my services," he added. "I know this is not the time or the place, but these matters must be dealt with."

Virgil felt the anger rise as he watched the exchange. His father had been in the grave less than five minutes and here was T.L. Gray haggling over his payment. "What a son-of-a-bitch," he said.

"Indeed," the voice answered. "You'll probably be happy to know that some people don't make it past the holding room," he added. "Some people don't even get there."

"Serves him right," Thompson replied. "But that still doesn't excuse the way I lived my life," he added.

"There is more," the voice said.

As he watched the people leave the cemetery, Thompson found himself remembering more and more about that day, including what happened next. There, looking back, about to enter a separate limousine, were his siblings . . . his sisters. "They were so small," he remarked.

He remembered it all. One of his sisters, Mandy, could barely walk. Another, Susan, was in diapers, and a third, little Sylvie, was in the arms of a woman he recognized as his aunt. She was the woman who placed the flower on the grave.

"There was five of us," he said. "Me and my four sisters," he added. "We was a handful. I remember it now."

As he watched, his grandfather came toward the small child who had been handed the flag and firmly shook his hand.

"That was me!" Virgil proclaimed proudly.

"You are the man of this family now," his Grandfather said.

"That's right; I was the man of the family . . ."

Young Virgil then turned to face his siblings once more. "He was the man of the family." They were words that struck a chord. His father told him that each time before he left for war.

"You're my little man," he remembered his father saying. "You watch over the house until I get home." When he returned home he would ask, "Did you take care of things while I was gone?"

"I was the man of the house," he mouthed. "I was the man of the . . . ."

"You were not. You were a child," the voice interrupted. "Like all little boys you believed the impossible was possible.

You believed that men could fly, and bullets could be stopped by puffing out your chest. That is the way of a child. But the truth was you were not a man. You were a small child who was hurting. You were a little boy who had just lost his father, who was now forced to live with your grandfather . . . without ever asking why. You were in pain."

"That's right," Virgil said. "I never did ask anyone why we went with Granddad that day. What did happen to my mother?"

"She was there are the funeral, but you didn't see her. That is why you did not remember the woman with the rose until now. The death of your father destroyed her emotionally. It happened a lot during that war. Here she was, barely grown herself with four children to raise and no way to support them. She had a nervous breakdown shortly after the funeral. That is why your grandfather and grandmother raised you. Your mother spent time in and out of mental institutions until she finally took her own life. You never knew because you were never told . . ."

"They said she was killed in a car accident . . ."

"She took an overdose of drugs. She died clutching your picture and that of your siblings . . ."

"My mother took her life?"

"She did . . ."

"And my siblings?"

"They were raised by your grandparents. It was either that, or the family would be split up and placed for adoption. The younger ones would have been easy to place but your older sisters would have been separated.

"But they were my responsibility," Virgil added. "I was the man of the family."

"You were not the man of any family. You were a child in a family torn apart by war. You were a victim, just like your mother."

Slowly the scene at the funeral began to fade. The casket that was being lowered into the ground was replaced by soil that had grown over the grave and grass where there once was dirt. The cars faded and other cars for other funerals appeared. Virgil found himself in another time and place altogether. "How do you do that?"

"We are in a place where time and space no longer matter," the voice explained.

This time, as he looked on, Virgil saw himself as a little boy, on the other side of a door trying to wedge his way outside to play. He remembered the screen and the white cottage trim that he had pulled apart. He remembered the rusted screen, and the holes the flies managed to navigate making their way inside. He found the flies to be unforgettable. As he looked down, he saw where his own initials had been painted over that summer. "V.T." he mouthed. And then he remembered why he was trying so desperately to get out. His best friend was knocking.

"Grandma," can I go out and play?" he asked. But he heard nothing in response, just the muffled cries of a woman who seemed to be in the other room, not far from the opening of the door. It sounded like a woman who was in the throes of a savage attack. Then he heard the breaking of glass and more muffled cries. He knew exactly what was happening. Again Virgil felt the anger of an innocence betrayed.

"Why'd he hit her like that?" he asked. "She never done nothin to him to deserve nothing like that. He beat the shit outta her."

"Again," the voice began. "All in life is ever as it seems . . . ."

"You're gonna tell me that that old lady wasn't getting' her ass kicked . . ."

"No I am not. She was being beaten . . ."

"And you didn't do a damn thing to stop it . . ."

"I can't intervene every time something goes wrong . . ."

"But you should have . . . ."

"Perhaps you're right, but there is more to the story than you know. Like your father, your grandfather was a veteran. And not unlike your father he did not return home . . . how would you put it . . . whole. His war was World War I. It was the first of what you called the war to end all wars. He fought hard in that war and returned home a hero but no one wanted to help him heal his wounds . . . ."

"Hero?"

"He saved the lives of his entire unit, but he paid an awful price. In his war the enemy used chemical weapons without prejudice. Many of those who died suffered horribly in their last moments of life. Those who lived, like your grandfather, bore psychological scars so deep that they never healed. Your grandmother remembered the man who went off to war and the hero who returned home emotionally wounded. She suffered through those beatings because she loved your grandfather until the day he died. That is not to say that she did not suffer through each of those attacks. She did. And so she too drank to hide her own pain. But make no mistake about it; they never blamed each other . . ."

"And then they had all us kids . . . my father's kids. They had to take care of us as well . . ."

"And they never once blamed you. Your grandmother knew that if she called the police on your father, you kids would be taken way. They saw you kids as a gift from God and nothing else. Any shortcomings they had they blamed themselves for. They didn't take it out on any of you kids. They just wanted you to get a better education so that you could get out of the cycle of misery your family found itself caught up in . . ."

"And I blew it . . . I remember em preachin all the time about goin to school," Virgil began by way of explanation. "But I didn't want nothin' to do with all that education stuff . . ."

"You had help. The devil works in strange ways. He introduces *doubt* where there should be *faith* and *anger* where there should be *calm,"* the voice explained. "Remember graduation day?"

"Yeah that's the day that son-of-a-bitch who *called* himself my best friend walked away with all of them honors. He had scholarships to go everywhere . . . . once again affirmative action. The niggers got all the shit," Virgil answered angrily, then sensing another embarrassing point was about to be made he started to calm down. "I mean Negroes."

"Perhaps you forget that *he* sat inside the same classroom that *you* sat in. You forget that *he* was black in a world sharply divided along lines of race. You forget that the teacher who gave *him* those straight A's was white, as was the principal and the schools that sought him out. They weren't looking at the color of his skin; they were looking at his test scores. Correct me if I am wrong, but you sat together during the test . . ."

"He was always smarter than I was . . ."

"Smarter? He struggled just like you did . . . . which is why he always came to your house for help with his . . ."

"History!"

"Exactly."

For the first time in what seemed to be an eternity, Virgil smiled. "He couldn't figure out which was which, the Revolutionary War or the Civil War. He was real stupid when it came to History," Virgil offered up proudly. "He especially hated all that European crap that they taught. I guess you could say I helped him get through those classes."

"And he helped you with math. If the two of you had continued to work together instead of apart, the world was your footstool. Instead you allowed small defeats to grow into larger ones. You allowed petty differences to grow into major disputes. You forgot he was in the same boat as you were. You were both poor trying to escape your circumstances. But instead of seeing a friend your views were colored by the doubt that entered your own mind. You began to doubt your own abilities and blamed him for your shortcomings. You were the one who allowed the color of his skin to color your viewpoint of the world . . ."

"Yeah but his parents . . ."

"They washed dishes on the weekends at the local Country Club just to make ends meet," the voice interrupted. "They studied with their children the same way your grandparents studied with you. His father had less than an eighth grade education. His mother finished one year in college and had to quit school to take care of *her* father who was just returning home from war. When he returned home, he was forced to sit in the back of a bus by people whose lives he fought to protect. We all have our crosses to bear."

"But affirmative action . . . the way they tried to fix it . . . that wasn't right!" Thompson snapped back.

"Neither was the fact that the dishes his parents washed were the dishes your Grandparents left behind at the local Moose Lodge at Christmas. His father was allowed to wash their dishes, but not allowed to eat in the dining room. He could serve his fellow veterans but not eat alongside them. And even though he too was a veteran of a foreign war, he was no more welcome at the local VFW, than he was in the back of the bus . . ."

"That wasn't my fault!"

"None of it was. The key is in recognizing that your cross is not your prison. Sometimes our greatest curses only serve to make us stronger . . . Gandhi used a nation's hunger to prove his point. His hunger strikes crippled the British resolve. The Reverend Dr. Martin Luther King chose non-violence. The harder his oppressors hit him, the stronger he and his movement became. All great men are faced with a time that they have to make impossible choices. You, like he, had a choice. Sometimes adversity is nothing more than a test . . ."

"And I failed . . . ."

"Not yet! I and only I determine when there is nothing left to learn."

"So there's hope?"

"There is always hope."

Chapter twenty-seven

T he holding room was dark once more. So dark it numbed the sense of sight and heightened all other senses. Smell was assaulted the most. "What's that?" Suleiman Muhammad asked as he awoke to find himself surrounded by what appeared to be the bloodied remains of . . . people! "The smell is sickening!" he said as he promptly began to vomit.

Each body appeared to be in various stages of decomposition. It was as if he were standing inside the morgue of all humanity . . . a place that housed the remains of everyone who had ever died throughout history. The stench was overwhelming. And there were flies . . . thousands of flies. Still it was the smell that was the worst. It was an awful stench that almost caused him to vomit. There were thousands of bodies, as far as the eyes could see. There were bodies of men and women, Asian and African, European and American. But one body in particular stood out. There, frozen, just as he and the others had been when Suleiman awakened, was a man who appeared to be a Japanese soldier. His hands were held high, as if surrendering.

Across his forehead was a silk scarf with the red rising sun emblazoned in the middle.

It was vintage World War II but the man appeared much older than a soldier in battle. Instead it looked as if he had surrendered long after the war had ended. His uniform sagged where it should have fit snugly and was tattered and disheveled. His face showed the wrinkles of countless nights of worry.

He was old. He was much older than a soldier who died in his youth.

"Where am I?" Suleiman asked.

"I call this my hall of martyrs," the voice answered.

"Martyrs?" Muhammad asked.

"Yes . . . these are the thousands of men and women, all of whom died for their individual beliefs. They died fighting for a cause that most of humanity has long since forgotten. The people who they left behind believe that they were greeted by hundreds of virgins or some other great honor when they got to heaven. The problem is . . . most of the people before you didn't believe in heaven. They worshiped some other god who didn't guarantee anything even remotely resembling the afterlife. It seems to have been a religious *typo* if you ask me. After all how can you believe in something *after* death, if you don't believe in life once you get there? So in short I gave them what they asked for. They are here and they are dead. For the rest of the world I sent my son Jesus, remember?"

"We thought of Jesus as a prophet in my religion, but nothing more than that."

"And you were wrong."

"What about him?" Muhammad asked pointing to the Japanese soldier. "How did he die?"

"Oh yeah, Takei, the last Samurai . . . he died believing in his cause during World War II. They found him in a cave long after the war was over. He was there, holding his position waiting to be relieved. That day never came. Instead, when he was discovered, it was by tourists who came to see the sight of one of World War II's worst battles. They found him and his antiquated beliefs. He believes in Buddha and has been here since long after the war waiting for Buddha to pick him up," the voice answered with a detectable note of sarcasm. "Sadly . . . still no word from Buddha . . . ."

"And him?" Muhammad asked, pointing to a bloodied pile of what was once someone. There was the faint appearance of what seemed to be and eye ball and a partial hand. The skull appeared to have collapsed inward, leaving little of what used to be the brain cavity. Flies feasted on the flesh of whoever he or she once was.

"Beats the hell out of me," the voice answered, pausing for a moment and then laughing out loud. "I get a kick out of that phrase. Beats the *hell* out of me . . . you humans have such cute expressions. Think about it, if you could beat the hell out of someone we would be pounding on just about everyone,"

Again the laughter . . . an awkward pregnant pause. "Oh yeah, now back to him. I don't know *who* he is. I can't even recognize him. Can you?"

Muhammad looked at the pile of rotting flesh and shook his head no.

"*He* might even be a *she*. That's the problem with all this martyr stuff. By the time your soul gets here, I can't figure the bodies out. You think *your* cremation created a problem. That's nothing compared to blowing yourself up. It makes for one hell of a mess. That's why I created this side room off of the holding room. Every once in a while someone gets the idea that dying for a cause is noble. If you think about that too long it will cause your brain to freeze. Dying for a cause means one thing and one thing only, dying. The greatest gift I gave to you was life itself. Nothing can be more precious. That's why men should think twice, and then forty more times before taking their own or anyone else's life. There are no second chances. The cause usually goes on without you. Got so many people at one time it started to stink up the joint. I had people fighting so long in Northern Ireland; generations forgot what they were fighting for."

"And them . . ."

"Proves my point. That thar's the Hatfield and McCoys," the voice replied trying to mock a terribly over-pronounced southern accent. "Their blood feud began over a pig . . . a pig mind you . . . ."

"Yeah I read about that in my history books . . . ."

"And so did your kids . . . and their kids . . ."

"But they were Christians . . ."

"I know . . . I just like to leave them here as a conversation point. Some people give up on heaven and spend their entire lives in hell," the voice answered. "That's what happens when people sacrifice the most precious gift of all, life, for a cause."

"Is that where I would have wound up?" Muhammad asked.

"No it's not. I guess the best way to describe how things work is by stating the obvious. You're still here," the voice answered. "Last time I checked *Christianity* isn't anywhere near your religious title. I got a spot for you right over there next to old "Takei,"" he continued. "You might want to consider that fact when you think about playing soccer with your little brother in heaven," the voice continued. "As always the choice is yours. I'd take a couple of minutes to think about it."

Muhammad looked around the room. If there were such a place as hell, this was it. Several of the bodies were in such states of decomposition their flesh had fallen from the bones. In addition, the flies, he now noticed, were larger than any flies he had ever seen. Indeed, they seemed to be well fed. And then there was old "Takei." How long had he been there, frozen in place? Muhammad realized that his religion got complicated when it came to the afterlife. He realized he had spent most of his religious life thinking of hate, as opposed to love, revenge as opposed to living life itself even though his own Koran said otherwise.

Then the thought of an eternity hit him. He thought about the possibility of never seeing his precious brother again. That thought seemed unbearable. Yet, he didn't want to appear to be a hypocrite to God, of all people. What would God think if he switched religions simply because it was convenient at the time?

"Kinda perplexing isn't it?" the voice asked as if reading his mind. "Pick one God and you get 72 virgins. Pick another and you get a life in eternal bliss . . . easy on the surface but kind of hard when you realize there are no guarantees . . . what if your religion is wrong?"

"You got that right . . ."

"That's the way I made it. Think about it, if everyone *knew* where they were going they wouldn't show up at church on Sunday. Bad enough most people only get dressed up for Easter and Christmas. If heaven were guaranteed they wouldn't even show up then. That's why I made religion a tough decision. Still, once you make up your mind it's pretty easy to get in. All you have to do is accept Jesus Christ as your lord and savior . . ."

"Did my brother make the choice?"

"He didn't have to. He was an innocent child caught up in the violent world around him. He didn't have time to think about what religion he wanted before that bomb went off. He's like all the other innocent bystanders caught up in someone else's war. Would have been kinda cruel for me to punish him, now wouldn't it?" the voice inquired.

"I guess I can see you logic," Muhammad answered. "I'm glad you spared him . . ."

"Most people do see my logic sooner or later," the voice answered sarcastically. "Most people . . . now if you don't mind I've got some other business to take care of. I'll be back," he said.

"What about me?"

"Talk to Takei! He's got nothing but time on his hand. But I gotta warn you, he ain't much for conversation!"

Chapter twenty-eight

"Mr. God," Virgil began sheepishly, "might I have a moment of your time."

"I have been here for you all along," the voice answered.

"There's been something I been dying to ask you," he paused for a moment, reflected upon the unintended humor in his question, and continued. "Some things just don't make sense . . ."

"Like what?"

"We'll this sin thing," Virgil began. "I been doin some thinking and it seems that we . . . I mean us humans . . . shouldn't bear all the blame . . . you know what I'm saying?"

"Sadly I do," the voice continued. "It is one of the most frequently asked questions when people get to heaven . . . ."

"So you know what I'm gonna ask?"

"Think about it while I answer. You want to know why, if I am omniscience, as I am, do I allow bad things to happen . . ."

Virgil interrupted. "Yeah . . . that's it exactly. Seems we're human but *you're* God. All you have to do is to twist your nose . . ."

"You've been watching too much TV . . ."

"Whatever . . . but you get my point. All you have to do is throw down a lightning bolt and all wars would stop and we would start getting along . . . you know?"

Has it ever dawned on you just how boring life would be if everyone got along? You argue over how you look, how much you weigh, how much money you make, who has the bigger house, fastest car and who comes from the best race . . ."

"Yeah but if you got rid of all that stuff we wouldn't be fightin' an stuff.."

"Yes you would!"

"Why?"

"Because it's in your nature. I created man to be able to create and solve problems. It is not I who tells you to take the easy path. I gave man the Garden of Eden and he ate the apple. I am not the God of deceit, or lies, or mistrust. If I took way your ability to choose you would be no different than the animals, and God knows . . . ," the voice paused, to reflect on his own feeble attempt at humor, "I have enough things around here to take care of."

"So you can't really blame us humans for getting' into so much trouble," Virgil offered by way of lame excuse. "I mean after all, you could have stopped any of us anytime we made mistakes. We woulda' learned before any harm was done . . ."

"No you would not have . . ."

"I beg to differ . . ."

"And you may, someplace else, but the evidence is stacked against you. You have been fighting wars because of your inability to solve things for years. Take a look through this door . . ."

Virgil walked toward the door that appeared out of nowhere. "Where did this come from?"

"I'm full of surprises," the voice answered. "Now open the door."

Virgil turned the knob. The smell was of musk and mold and quickly assaulted his senses. It smelled . . . old. "How old is this room?" he asked.

"Three thousand years give or take a few centuries," the voice answered. "I call it my crusades wing."

"Them guys look like knights and stuff, you know King Arthur and them round table dudes."

"Yes that was the *phrase* that escaped me . . . them round table dudes . . ." he said sarcastically.

"But I though they was the good guys."

"I thought you might find them familiar. Do you think that yours was the first to think that they were doing right in the name of my Son? These men marched off into battle carrying the symbol of his death on the cross. That, they believed, would protect them in battle. Did they not think it hypocritical to march off into war in the name of a man who dedicated his life to the cause of peace?"

Virgil suddenly began to fidget. The sheets and hood that had been missing since his death reappeared, as if by magic. Now, standing before God, he looked his worse. He looked like hate!

"Look at you, you fool. You wear sheets and hoods to hide your face, and yet you say you are there to defend those who cannot defend themselves. Then you do battle, in the name of Jesus Christ, arguing that you are against race mixing. Your geographic ignorance alone staggers the imagination. Did you think that Christ looked as if he sat in the front row of a NASCAR race with a six pack in his hands drinking beer with the good ol' boys? This was a man from Nazareth, or what you now call the Middle East. If nothing else, he looks more like those you would call your enemy than your friends . . ."

"But we was fightin . . ."

"And that says it all . . . you were *fightin*. That is all men do. You were *'fightin'* for what . . . peace . . . prosperity . . . equality? My son said turn the other cheek forty times forty and then again. How many times did you turn the other cheek before you lashed out against those who were different than you? Your wars were not for racial purity or for that matter anything that had to do with any religion that was taught anywhere. Yours was a battle based on pure hatred because one man looked different than you. My son taught love. You preached hate and it will haunt you into the afterlife!"

"But you could have stopped it!"

"And that is what I am doing now!"

Virgil wanted to rip the sheets from his body. Their mere presence produced a burning sensation as if the very clothes themselves were on fire. The more he struggled the tighter the robes became. He was suffocating, drowning in his own hate . . . his every word past and presence was being used against him before the almighty.

"Look around you Virgil, and tell me what do you see? Do you see your friends, or for that matter the people you call your enemies? This is my hall of hate. If you look closely you will see that all wars begin with the same elements, jealousy, hatred, betrayal. And if you look even closer you will notice that nowhere to be found, are the men who actually decided to go to war. No Virgil, the reason man fights is because he is foolish. He never believes that he will one day stand before me in judgment as you are now. I could have stopped it all at any moment . . . and so could you. The difference is, I am judge, and you are about to be judged!"

Chapter twenty-nine

"Little Peggy" walked toward her mother's bedroom. The first board on the third step creaked as it always did. The rail at the top wobbled when she placed her hand atop it, as it always did. She was hoping that when she opened the door her mother would be sitting there waiting for her morning paper as she always did. Instead, when she opened the door, there was nothing but silence. So, as she had done every morning for the last five years, she entered and placed the newspaper atop the nightstand as she had done so many times before. Glancing down she realized that the headlines never changed. It was all about hate. Someone died, someone argued and someone divorced. "God must cry when he sees this," she said softly.

Interspersed with the stories about the death of Suleiman Muhammad and the right Reverend Eugene Kinney, there was a story about how peace negotiations in the Middle East collapsed because a member of the Arab delegation refused to shake hands with a member of the Israeli delegation. In the moments that followed the member of the Arab delegation suffered a massive heart attack.

The Israeli delegation proclaimed it was a sign from God.

There was also a story about a local minister who had done well. He had taken his fortune and in the biblical sense, took up his cross. The story was short and begged for more in the way of detail. None was found.

"This seems out of place," she said, as she read the article. "Pastor James Graham leaves it all behind to help the starving in Africa," the article read. She remembered hearing about Graham. He was a man who not only walked the walk but talked the talk. A former military man, he made a fortune and then decided to leave it all behind so that he could spend the rest of his days helping the less fortunate. "Clearly God will find room for him," she said.

As she glossed over the headlines, "Little Peggy" longed for the days that she would sit by her mother's bedside and share the newspaper together. Her mother always read the front page, followed by the other segments of the paper in order. Then, neatly folded, she would hand them to "Little Peggy" for further review. It had been that way since she was a little girl. "Little Peggy" chose to skip the meatier segments of the paper and headed straight to the comics. There was, she assumed, plenty of time to get serious about life.

As she grew older, her tastes in reading changed. Soon she was reading the entire newspaper just like her mother and her father until he passed away. Today was no different. One headline in particular leapt from the pages of the paper.

Like the comics, it was in the entertainment segment, but unlike the comics, it was no laughing matter. It involved the story of a rapper who went by the name of "The Great White Hope" who was shot as he left a Los Angles nightclub. She had heard about it on the news. Doctors marveled that he was still alive after dying three times on the operating room table. The headline read . . .

"Hope clinging to life support"

"How sad," she remarked.

Scanning the room, she looked for comfort in the familiar. There were the customary photos of the family scattered atop the dressers and nightstand. A small plastic box, yellowed with time, had a letter indicating the day of the week across the top. Inside the box were the pills that had become her mother's daily regimen. The telephone sat next to the box, and the TV remote sat next to the phone which was positioned underneath the lamp. Next to the phone was a smaller box that housed a portable cellular phone still in its wrapping waiting to be programmed. The VCR atop the TV still flashed 12 blinking on and off as it had since the last storm. Just above the television was the clock.

"It stopped," she said realizing that the second had no longer continued its rounds. Instead the clock was stopped at 7:39, the exact moment of her mother's death. "I'll be dammed," she said before realizing what she had just uttered. "Hopefully not," she added.

Chapter thirty

"Your Excellency," Virgil Thompson began. He next cleared his throat in a loud guttural sound. But God was not listening. Instead he was singing.

"And she's buying me a stairway to heaven," he sang in a shrill voice. Turning he noticed Virgil Thompson standing there. "I just love that song, but the lyrics don't make much sense," he added. "I mean think about it. Anyone attempting to climb a stairway to heaven would spend their entire lives getting here. You think Mars is far. Wait until you start out on that journey! And the way most of your live your lives you would collapse long before getting here. That doesn't make any senses now does it?" he asked.

"I guess not," Thompson replied.

"And another thing, what is a 'bustle in a hedgerow'? Been trying to figure that one out for years . . ."

"Yeah I know," Thompson answered. "They played that song at my prom. Decorated the gym up and all, made it real pretty," he continued.

"And yet you didn't go," the voice replied.

"That thing was for losers," Thompson answered.

"My point indeed," the voice added sarcastically. "So why didn't you go?"

"I get it . . ."

'So what was it you wanted?" the voice asked.

"I was wondering if there was something I could do to change your mind about where I might be headed," he asked. "I would do anything . . ."

"I know . . . anything for one more chance. Boy that's original. I haven't heard that one before. Remember that time you went drinking in that bar down on Chapline Street?"

"You remember that?"

"I never forget. You almost killed yourself you were so drunk. If it hadn't been for that deer you would have slammed into a tree about a quarter of a mile down the road . . ."

'That sobered me up," Thompson added. "Damned thing scared me half to death,' he continued.

"That deer saved your life," the voice answered. "I heard your prayers. If I remember it correctly, it went something like this . . . God if you just help me to get home I promise to live a better life . . ." Then the voice continued sarcastically. "If I only had a nickel for each time I heard that prayer."

"I remember saying it," Thompson said.

"But did you live it?" the voice asked. 'How long were you sober that time? Did it not occur to you that each and every time you picked up a bottle and placed it before your lips, you continued a cycle that haunted you to your grave?"

"I guess not . . ."

"And how did you thank that the deer that saved your life?" The voice asked.

"What, you wanted me to invite him over for dinner?"

"No I expected you to show compassion for all things living," the voice answered. "Instead, each and every thanksgiving you didn't invite him over for dinner. He *was* dinner. You and your friends loaded up the truck and headed out in the fall drinking and shooting anything and everything in sight. There is enough food in grocery stores around the world and yet you felt the need to kill . . ."

"We was just huntin' . . ."

"I have long toyed with the possibility of a room just for animals and their hunters . . . only the rules would differ slightly," the voice said. "Imagine what it would feel like if the deer had the guns and you were the prey . . ."

'Wouldn't be too fair . . . I guess," Virgil answered sheepishly, stumbling for an answer. "I guess it's a good thing that deer can't shoot," he added trying to lighten a situation that was growing increasingly awkward. "A whole lot of us would be dead."

"And yet you stand before me at the precipice between heaven and hell wondering how to take the next step. That's the problem with man. You treat eternity as if it is something that be traded for. This is not a time for you to bargain. This is a time for you to listen and to repent. I would suggest you do so . . ."

"I'm working on it," Thompson answered. Instead he was met with silence. God had his headsets on and was singing once more.

"And she's buying me a stairway to heaveeeennnnn . . . ."

Chapter thirty-one

"Please take a seat," the nurse said. "We have some paperwork to fill out and then we can begin the procedure," she suggested.

The little girl sat clutching the small clipboard she had been handed and slowly checked off the answers. Are you at least 18 years of age? She checked box saying yes. It was a lie. As she checked off each box on the form she scanned the room to see if anyone was watching. It was instinct. The room was small, no more than twelve feet in any direction. There was a cabinet filled with what appeared to be medical supplies. There were jars filled with cotton balls and tongue depressors. In the middle of the room, the table with shiny metal stirrups that seemed so menacing close up. The air was sterile, thick, and growing more and more difficult to breath. It smelled of formaldehyde.

"The procedure will take less than twenty minutes," the nurse explained in a callous, I have done this so many times before voice. "Are you ready?" She asked.

"Say no," Peggy Wilson said under her breath as she watched it all. "Please, for the love of God say no!" She already knew it was too late.

Instead the little girl signed her name across a line at the bottom of the first page of lies and gently placed the clipboard on the small night table by her side. The clipboard in place, she reached down and pulled a small wallet from her purse. Reaching inside, she pulled from it a small rolled up wad of cash. Then she began to count. "Twenty . . . forty . . . ." And so on until she reached $360.00. "I believe that is the amount you told me to bring," she explained, handing the money to the nurse.

"I don't want to watch this," Peggy Wilson said softly as her pleas fell upon deaf ears.

"What you are about to see has already occurred," the voice explained. "It is your past."

"But we both know what happens . . ."

There was silence. A deafening silence unlike any Peggy Wilson had ever experienced. Even though it had already happened, her eyes were transfixed by the events about to unfold.

"Every time I watch this I ask myself the same question," the voice said. "How can anyone do this? How can anyone take the life of a tiny child?"

"I didn't think I had a choice . . ."

"There is always a choice . . . it is never about choice," the voice continued. "It is about a decision. That is where man strays."

"Please, if you would," the nurse said in almost whispered tones, "remove all of your clothes and put this on. You can fold them and place them on this chair. No one will disturb them, I promise." She handed the little girl a small bloodstained smock for her to drape herself in. "The doctor will be in, in a moment," she added and then backed away a few steps at a time before turning and starting to walk out the door.

"Will I feel anything," the girl asked causing the nurse to pause in mid step.

"Not for $360," the nurse answered a somewhat scolding tone. "You won't feel a thing," she added sarcastically. "*You* won't feel a thing!"

The little girl waited . . . naked underneath the smock for what seemed to be an eternity. A small analogue clock with a white face and black sweeping second hand ticked away in the corner of the room. It was positioned just above the medicine cabinet filled with the cotton swabs and tongue depressors.

"Tick . . . tick . . . . tick . . . ." with each passing second the girl's eyes grew wider. The tension in the room grew even more pronounced. "Tick . . . tick . . . tick . . ." Twice, she rose, as if she wanted to leave the room and twice she sat down. Each time she took her seat she was more and more unsettled. Then there was the smock. It was too small and barely covered the areas she wanted to keep private. Still she mused at how trivial her own privacy seemed when she was about to sell her soul.

Within minutes the room came alive with the sound of a small suction pump. To be so small, the noise was deafening. The little girl's eyes seemed transfixed on the motion of the pump, as the small ballast inside pulsated up and down. She was now sitting up, her legs spread wide in the stirrups. The doctor entered the room. She paid little attention to his face, which was hidden behind a surgical mask. Only his eyes could be seen, and they were hidden behind a thick pair of black framed glasses. But it wasn't his well hidden face, but instead the iciness in his voice that caused her the most discomfort.

"How'd 'ya' get knocked up?" he asked coldly. He seemed more like a doctor, priest and gossip all rolled into one. He was black, perhaps Hispanic, and perhaps Asian. Unlike other doctor's offices she had been in, there were no proud diplomas lining these walls. In fact if she had to prove he was a doctor, she could not. He could just as well been an auto mechanic, for all she cared. "Boyfriend? Father? That's okay . . . I don't want to know . . . ."

Then the room went silent. The doctor, the little girl, and the pump were all frozen in time.

Peggy Wilson's eyes were focused on a small baby she hadn't seen before. It was an infant huddled in the far corner of the holding room. The child was pale in appearance, with no discernible featured other than his eyes . . . those haunting eyes. The baby, no more than three or four months old, was talking.

"I can remember the warmth . . . the voices . . . the love . . . and yes I can remember the happiness," the child began. "I can also remember the darkness." Then turning and facing Peggy Wilson the small child continued, "I was there you know. I was there the whole time. You could not see me, or hear me but I could you. I heard your every conversation. I was there every time . . ."

Peggy Wilson could see the pained expression on the face of the child as he continued. The lines across his forehead were so pronounced for the child to be so young. He gestured with tiny hands that seemed so innocent, and yet so expressive. And in that that instance, he seemed tired. He seemed old.

"I remember everything before . . . during and after that day. I heard your joy when you learned you were pregnant and I felt your pain when fear replaced joy. I experienced your sadness . . . your tears. I remember it all," the tiny child added.

Peggy Wilson was crying uncontrollably. Puddles of tears formed beneath her feet as she clutched her sides and bent over in shame. "Please stop!" she cried. "I don' want to hear anymore. I'm so sorry! I'm so very sorry," she sobbed. "I was a child myself . . . I was just like you! I made a mistake!"

But the child continued as if not hearing a single word that Peggy Wilson had uttered in her moment of protest. "I was there for the bright light and the sudden stillness that followed. I was there for the cold . . . the icy unbearable cold!"

The child's words were interrupted by the sound of the pump . . . that horrible sound. Everything in the room was moving again. Peggy Wilson looked down as the liquid inside the jar attached to the pump, merged with the flow of blood and turned into ribbons of crimson red. She could smell the formaldehyde. She could see her own shame on the face of a child she had long ago buried in the recesses of her subconscious mind. She could see the callous expression on the face of the doctor as he began the procedure. She watched as he moved the tiny metal wand slowly from side to side . . . sucking the very life itself from between her legs . . . she could taste her tears.

"Then . . . there was the icy unbearable cold," the infant continued with a haunting tone in his voice. ". . . . the icy unbearable cold!"

Peggy Wilson, watching it all, began thrashing about in much the same manner a wild animal would upon being cornered and caged. In that moment she was that animal . . . under the control of something larger . . . far more powerful. With each insertion of the surgical probe by the doctor, the precious moments of her own life flashed before her and spilled into the background of the holding room. Now there was only the little girl, the doctor, the pump and her memories.

With each insertion she screamed a single word, "Nooooo!!!"

Then as her cries echoed through the holding room there was only silence. The scene changed.

She next saw herself as a wounded child wandering through life aimlessly. She saw herself coming home to parents who wondered what happened to cause her to become so distant. She saw the first Christmas following the procedure and how she stared off into space while the rest of the family celebrated. She saw her next birthday, and the one after that . . . until the family stopped celebrating because she stopped smiling. She saw the Christening of her best friend's baby and how she cowered in the corner of a restroom in the back of the church afterwards in tears. She saw her icy resolve grow as the event inside the abortion clinic grew further and further away.

She saw how that single moment transformed a frightened little girl into a callous and confused and angry woman. It changed her life. Every decision made since then was because of the guilt she suffered. She remembered her thoughts when she joined the choir in her church. She should have been singing songs of celebration. Instead her thoughts raced back to the event inside the clinic. The same happened when she joined the deacon board . . . when she accepted Christ . . . when she married . . . when she had her first *wanted* child.

She remembered the fear in wondering whether God would curse she and her husband because of what *she* had done. She remembered her own shame upon being told *her* daughter, the one who carried her name, was barren and could not have children. She remembered hanging her head in shame and silently telling herself, "It was God's will."

She heard the sound.

It sounded so familiar.

Slowly the doctor reached over and pushed a small red button on the side of the device. The pump stopped as did Peggy Wilson's thrashing.

She was spent.

There was no more fighting and no one to fight with. Whatever it was that had gripped her, had won. She glanced downward at the child in the clinic . . . a vulnerable child, afraid and cowering in the sterile confines of an abortion clinic. She was alone. The jar was filled with the lifeless soul of a person who would never be. She knew then that when she underwent the procedure that day, a part of her soul disappeared inside a tiny jar that was placed outside later that night with the trash.

She died.

She realized that hers was not a choice at all, but instead, a death sentenced carried out for *two* people. A small child died that day as did a young girl who would spend the rest of her life living with the shame. She realized that no matter how many times she may have told herself differently, it was never about the choice; instead it was always about the child. She realized she had chosen, and she had chosen wrong.

The little girl shivered in the corner of the clinic. She barely opened her eyes as she gathered herself and began to put her clothes back on. Only once did she open them long enough to dare to steal a parting glance at the doctor as he prepared to leave the room. She watched as he stood erect and proud, as if nothing had happened. She watched as he removed the white rubber surgical gloves that were stained with her blood, and the blood of her unborn child and walked out of the room as if it were just another day at the office.

He had been paid in full.

She paid with her soul.

The *child*, however, was far from finished.

Chapter thirty-two

The baby, rising above the corner of the holding room, spoke once more. "Yes, I remember your words then. I remember your words when you first learned you were pregnant. They were harsh and bitter. The love in your heart turned to hate. Then I watched as the hate turned to action and at the end, as you can see, I was no more."

In a moment that seemed to last for an eternity, the child continued to rise. It was levitating, hovering in mid air, pressing his face against hers. He showed no expression, no emotion. Then he began to speak again. "It is the *words* that refuse to go away, the words that cut the deepest. I will never forget them. I can never forget your words."

Peggy Wilson knew that at that moment . . . that this was what judgment day was all about. It was about coming face to face with an ugly past she tried to bury through her years of church service. She wondered whether it was a child she was listening to, or the voice of God, or her own guilty conscience. It mattered little. She knew now she had been judged and found guilty of an unforgiveable sin. She had taken a human life . . . the life of a precious child . . . and found guilty. She had violated God's first commandment, "thou shall not kill!" All along she spent her days, from that moment on, hoping that God would forgive her. She prayed that the memory of that horrible day would somehow fade. Seeing it all come back to life, she knew now that God, like she, could never forget what happened that day. She knew he would never forgive her for what she had done.

Some sins, she realized, are too big to forgive. She had been judged . . . by the child she had abandoned. Her greatest evil was not being a skinhead, or member of the KKK or a renegade pastor. Her demon was a choice. She would spend the rest of eternity being haunted by the final words of a child whose life she cut short, *"I will never forget you . . . any of you!"*

Slowly all of the images began to fade. After a while, even the little girl, who cowered in the corner, was no more. The abortion clinic was gone, the doctor, the nurse and soon the child who hovered above her. It was then that Peggy Wilson began to understand what the holding room was all about.

When she first arrived she saw the others. She saw the Klan Grand Dragon, the man whose body was filled with outward signs of hate. She saw the crooked preacher. She had seen what she wanted to see, and ignored what she was supposed to see. She saw, as the preachers would say over and over again, the 'spec in the eye' of someone else, while ignoring the 'log' inside her own eye.

The baby was there, in the holding room, all along, waiting for his moment to speak. He was there when she first entered the holding room . . . just waiting. She was being judged by the one person in the room who could not speak for himself. The others were all extensions of what *she* had done. Her actions set in motion the events that shaped the lives of all those around her. The end result was a life unfulfilled that cascaded through time like the sound waves from an explosion. She knew that the ripple effect was far reaching and that the others were collateral damage from her own selfish decisions.

She was responsible for *them*. She was responsible for *him*. It took a child to bring it all to light.

Dropping to her knees, face down on a floor that was already stained with her tears, she began to pray. "Our father . . . who art in heaven . . . hallowed be thy name . . ." When she completed the prayer the first time, she began again . . . and again, and again. She prayed for forgiveness. She prayed for peace. She prayed for a second chance at life, or death, or whatever. She prayed until slowly, everything and everyone around her started to disappear. She was no longer praying for her own soul.

She was praying for theirs.

She belonged in the holding room.

They did not.

She prayed for their forgiveness.

Chapter thirty-three

"Mr. Thompson," the voice began, in a thunderous tone. "It is time."

Virgil Thompson felt his knees begin to shake. There was a tightening in his stomach that he hadn't felt since he was a small child. It was a sickening nauseous feeling reserved for the worst of all fears. He was about to be judged and he knew what the judgment would be. He had spent a lifetime sinning, and hating, and killing and time had run out. He knew that he was headed straight to hell. God was about to deliver the final blow to a life wasted. "Yes your highness," he replied.

"I want you to look at something," the voice replied.

The fear was quickly replaced by the realization that for the first time in his life, there was nothing left to fear. Every minute of his life had been laid bare. There was nothing left to hide. He knew it and he knew God knew it. He had seen the bad and the ugly; there was little that was good to be seen. He had seen it all. Now he was alone inside the holding room waiting for his final judgment.

As the image on the wall came into focus Thompson watched as a sleek Lincoln Town Car road through a line of towering oak trees and pulled up out in front of a church he recognized from his travels in and out of town. It was a wealthy church on the outskirts of town where people unlike him worshiped. The lawn was well manicured. The gardens were well kept. "What is this all about?" he asked.

"It is your funeral," the voice answered.

"I ain't had no funeral," Thompson replied defiantly, summoning what remained of his dignity. He vowed that if was to go straight to hell, he would do so with some semblance of pride intact.

"You were dead so how could you know?" the voice answered matter-of-factly. "Forgive me for pointing out the obvious, but once you are dead it matters little. You did have a funeral. You didn't know it. And this is where it was held . . ."

"I didn't go to that church . . ."

"You didn't go to *any* church . . . but *he* did." As the voice spoke the door to the Lincoln Town Car opened.

Virgil Thompson instantly recognized the man getting out. "What the hell is he doin at my funeral?" he asked. "Is he here to spit on my grave?"

"No . . ." the voice began. "There were plenty who wanted to spit on your grave. Then, as the days passed, they no longer cared. He is there because he paid for your funeral. He paid for every flower, every candle and the invitations that went out to your former friends. He made sure they all came . . . . even if he had to pay their cab fare out of his own pocket."

"But why?"

"Because he never forgot the sacrifices you made for him," the voice answered.

"Sacrifices?"

"Yes, sacrifices," the voice answered.

"I don't understand," Thompson answered.

"You usually don't," the voice replied. "For everything in life that happens there is a consequence both good and bad. You were the bad consequence to everything good that happened in his life . . ."

"I told you . . . affirmative action and all that stuff. He got rich off of me," Thompson answered. "Serves him right having to pay for my funeral . . ."

"He didn't *have* to pay for your funeral . . . he wanted to," the voice continued. "He remembered his friend who he played with growing up. He remembered the good times and how you helped him out with his history homework history. Because of what you did he silently set up a scholarship in your name to pay for tutoring young children who had difficulty with their history lessons," the voice continued. "He turned your hate into something good."

"But why?"

"Because it is written," the voice answered. "To whom much is given, much is required."

One by one they came until slowly the church filled. When the doors closed there were no seats to be found. The minister began the eulogy; Thompson took inventory of the crowd. "Whose kids are those?"

"They are his kids," the voice answered.

"I bet they had better things to do," Thompson chimed in.

"Children always do," the voice said. "But it is the responsibility of the parents to raise their children in the right manner. He wanted them to know that you two were once friends. He wanted them to understand that the people you step over on the way to the top will be there when you come back down the ladder of success. He wanted to teach them how to pray for their friends and their enemies."

"I guess he wasn't so bad after all," Thompson said. "Maybe I misjudged him."

"There is more," the voice answered. As he spoke the image of the funeral changed to reveal a bedroom. It was dark. The two people inside the room were kneeling to pray. A man was on one side of the bed and a woman was on the other side.

"That's his old lady and old man," Thompson added. "But what have they got to do with all of this?"

"For once, just listen," the voice answered before you speak. "They're praying."

"Father," the husband began. "I pray for all of those who are less fortunate than us and anyone foolish enough to believe that he or she could be more fortunate than our family . . ."

'But they was poor like us . . ."

"Please listen . . . ."

"There's a kid down the street," the husband continued. "He's a little kid who doesn't have much. We just found out that our child is going off to college. I don't know what you have in store for him, but he deserves no less. So tonight father, instead of praying for my own children, I want to pray for him . . ."

"He did that for me?" Thompson asked.

"They both did, on more occasions than you might imagine," the voice replied. "They prayed for you a lot. They remembered when you used to come over for dinner. They knew what was going on inside your house. He was a soldier too. Just because the world discriminated against him, didn't mean that he discriminated against the rest of the world."

"So why would someone who was discriminated against pray for someone like me?"

"It is written that you should do unto others as you would want them to do unto you," the voice answered. "They prayed that I would continue to bless them, but they always recognized their own shortcomings. In seeing those shortcomings they recognized that sometimes prayer was the only answer."

The scene changed once more to as if were fast forwarding to the end of the funeral. T.L. Gray approached the man who moments ago had exited the Town Car, and accepted an envelope. As he stood there Gray opened the envelope and began to count what seemed to be an endless series of one hundred dollar bills. When he was finished counting, he stuffed the money back inside the envelope and both men went their separate ways.

"So why did you show this to me?" Thompson asked.

"I bought you here because that man, you so despise, just purchased your ticket to heaven."

Chapter thirty-four

Peggy Wilson continued to pray nonstop until the holding room was no more. And then she prayed again. This time she prayed for the return of the light. She had seen enough of the darkness in her life. She prayed to the God that she had been taught to worship. She prayed to the God of forgiveness . . . and of love. She prayed for a miracle because that is what she had become to believe in. She prayed.

Then one by one . . . the miracles began to happen!

The shadowy figures that were ensconced in darkness moments ago were now starting to reappear. As the light in the room grew brighter, she prayed harder and harder. She prayed that God was listening. Not willing to take any chances, she continued to pray until each of the figures who were in the holding room, when she first arrived, slowly began to take shape. Then closing her eyes . . . she prayed the prayer she dared not hope to pray. She prayed that God would someone find the compassion to give her a second chance.

When she could pray no more, she slowly opened her eyes once more.

There standing the middle of the others, Dylan Walsh, the skinhead, held a small child with his arms outstretched. "I believe this is yours," he said softly.

Peggy Wilson looked upon the face of the child. He was angelic, pure. He was smiling back at her.

The voice continued, "Study the face of the child. Allow it to come into focus . . ."

Perplexed Peggy Wilson answered, "I have been looking at the child. It is not any of my children. I would know them all anywhere," she added.

"It will not appear familiar at first, but soon you will come to know it," the voice answered. "Look closer. You will come to know it as the child that was once your own. He lived inside you *before* you decided to end his life. He is *that* child! He is *your* child!"

The realization that the baby, the infant before her, was the child she abandoned caused Peggy Wilson to collapse into a shaking heap of a fragile woman worn down by the ages of just a few moments. She knew that what she had seen before were images from her past. She realized that the holding room was a place where past, present, and future all came together before God. At that moment she knew, she was not only being judged for her past, but for what happened to his future. "It happened so long ago," she said, the tears now flowing freely. "I had hoped . . . I prayed . . . ."

"You prayed that *I* would forgive. That part was easy . . . but to forget?" the voice said, taking on a professorial tone. We are not judged by one small action or what we did at the *end* of our lives but instead, for the mosaic our lives create. I know that you sang in the choir, and served as a deaconess, but I also knew you before you were formed inside your mother's womb!," the voice proclaimed. "You were part of a larger plan that, left unchecked, was as perfect as Adam and Eve in the Garden of Eden. Yes the child was yours, but it was not yours to take away or give back. As always children are gifts to be cherished. You took that for granted."

"And I paid dearly for my sins every day of my life!" she cried. "I paid! I paid dearly!"

"But it was not *I* who asked you to pay," the voice answered. "I am a *loving* God. I only asked you to confess your sins then and move on. This last test, this last journey, is not part of your punishment, but instead your enlightenment. Like the people whose lives you touched with what you did in the past, what did *not* happen in the future shaped lives far beyond your comprehension . . ."

"I don't understand . . ."

"Nor can any human being," the voice began by way of explanation. "Man was not made to understand the complex nature of God. I am alpha and omega and therefore responsible for the beginning and the end. The mother of Moses had no idea that the child being placed inside a basket of reeds would one day rule Egypt and deliver my commandments to the world. Joseph and Mary were vessels for something far greater. My plans are not for you to understand . . ."

"You will understand it better by and by . . ." Peggy Wilson mouthed, repeating the words to the hymn she had sung so often.

"And sometimes you won't" the voice added. "What you did with the latter part of your life was enough to earn your place in heaven. *You* have placed your soul in hell. Guilt is a tool of the devil. Forgiveness is divine . . . ."

"So would you forgive me?"

"I did so long ago," the voice said softly. "And so did he . . ."

"He . . ."

"Yes you would have had a little boy . . . a precious little boy with all five toes and fingers. He had his eyes and your kind smile. I had big things in store for him. The Christmas you mourned was to have been his celebration. Like all children he comes to the world with a blank slate. It is what you write on that slate that separates them from the other children who are born. Sadly, however, that will never be. You ended it all with one selfish, short-sighted decision . . ."

"So how will I ever know what would have been . . ."

"Most people live their lives without ever knowing the precious things I have in store for you. You get not because you ask not," the voice continued. "Time and time again you are told that I am like a parent. What parent wishes ill for their child? When you have truly repented, you will understand that no sin is too great to be forgiven, but you must first learn to forgive yourself."

"So will I get into heaven?" she asked softly. Wiping away what remained of the tears.

"You will see in due time my child, in due time . . ."

Chapter thirty five

"That took forever!" 'Little Peggy" declared, clutching the urn containing her mother's ashes. "Seems sad when you think of it," she added, examining the vestibule more closely. "A person's entire life winds up inside this small jar. Momma weighed about one hundred pounds when she died and there's not one hundred pounds of momma in this jar." Then she started laughing uncontrollably. She was laughing so hard a tear slowly slid down her cheek making it hard to discern whether she was happy or sad.

'What?" her husband asked. "What is so funny?"

"I was just thinking," 'Little Peggy began by way of explanation. "What if somehow this really isn't mom?" she questioned. "What if we got someone else's ashes? What if there is someone else in this urn?"

A puzzled expression appeared on her husband's face. He knew the recent days had been stressful and feared his wife was about to crack. He watched as she fought with T.L. Gray, and then the FBI before finally being allowed to collect her mother's ashes. It was too stress much for anyone to take. Death, in a matter of a few days, had proven to be crueler than life. "Who else do you think is inside that urn?" he asked.

"That's the point. When someone is buried you know everything that happens," she began. "You deliver the body to the funeral home and approve everything from what they wear to the casket they are buried in. Then there is a viewing with an open casket. You watch them close the casket and watch the pall bearers escort it form the church. Then at the cemetery you watch them lower it into the ground. Someone places a flower or the first shovel full of dirt on the casket and then it's over. There is no doubt who is inside and who is in the ground."

"So what makes you think it's any different with cremation."

"I did some reading . . ."

"And . . ."

"I didn't like what I read," she said. "I read that when someone is cremated, they have to wait until for the furnace to cool down and then they empty the ashes. Once that process is done they start all over again . . ."

"And your point . . ."

"My point is that this was T.L. Gray. If you believe those stories in the newspaper, then there's a good chance he didn't do anything by the book. That man could squeeze the last dime out of a dollar. Think about it, do you really think that he allowed the furnace to cool down each and every time? I think he put as many bodies in there as he could. Then he lit the match and left it up to God to sort out who is who . . ."

"You gotta point there. So you're saying that that might not be your mom in that urn?"

"That's exactly what I'm saying," she answered. "Mamma didn't want to be cremated anyway. She wanted a proper funeral." She clutched the urn tighter. "I hope that is you in there mamma, if not I hope you're happy wherever you are."

Her husband chimed in. "I hope you're not someone else!"

Chapter thirty-six

It was a hot summer day. The sound of the Pittsburgh Pirates could be heard on transistor radios on cars, with the men still inside them. The announcer excitedly pointed out that Roberto Clemente, the great Pirates outfielder, was at bat. The 'day lilies' were in full bloom and the sweet smell of forsythias filled the air. It was a pleasant mix of the freshness of life and the barbecue of a church picnic. Peggy Wilson was standing across the street from the Macedonia Baptist Church. She knew exactly when it was.

"Do you recognize the man driving the truck?" the voice asked.

Peggy Wilson started to feel the tears well up in her eyes once more. This time her guilt over the loss of a child was replaced by the intense hatred of betrayal. "I know what happened that day," she cried. "I never forgave him for what he did."

"But do you know *why* he did it?" the voice asked. "By now you must realize, from your time in the holding room that nothing happens in a vacuum. Life is like the ripples in a pond.

A small pebble produces waves that grow larger and larger until the tsunami they produce engulfs everything around them. When it is over, few remember the pebble, only the damage it caused."

"We never spoke about what happened that day. We never spoke of the bombing or what happened after it. No one in the community wanted to have anything to do with the people who carried it out," she answered.

"Not even you?" the voice asked. "You had nothing to say as well. Not even a word to the man who fathered your child?"

"That man . . . that monster was not the father of my child," she sobbed. "The man I fell in love with was kind and gentle. I loved him and he loved me. We didn't let the color of our skin blind us to the troubles that lie ahead, but the man I fell in love with would never do what he did on that day . . . ."

"That man . . . was as guilty of his sins are you were yours. That day was a fateful one for all involved. He was waiting for you to come around the corner that morning. He wanted to plead one more time for you to keep the child. He loved you more than he hated the rest of the community. As the minutes passed, he became more and more angry," the voice continued. "God, he reasoned, was taking away the one thing he cherished the most, his child. He was willing to battle racism with you by his side. He was willing to fight for his family!"

"So are you saying . . ."

"That's exactly what I am saying. The devil fills in the void that good people leave open for him to exploit. It was the devil who caused the problems with the first truck. That was the pebble in the pond. It created the need for another means of transportation. Had he been at the clinic that morning with you, he wouldn't have been in position to be needed by the others. Had that not happened, the bombing would not have occurred. You see, on that day there were others who were having second thoughts. That night, they confessed their sins before God in a church on the other side of town. They were waiting for a sign . . ."

"So if he had been with me . . ."

"He wouldn't have been on that corner, and the men would have taken that as *my* sign that what was about to happen was wrong. They would have assumed that a broke truck was a sign from God that what they were about to do was wrong. They were looking for a small glimmer of hope. They were looking for anything that might suggest that I had not abandoned them. In the moments before evil prevails that is usually the case. It is a small window that opens for doubt, allowing hate to rush in. As a result the men believed there would be no sign . . . they took it the other way and proceeded."

Without warning Peggy Wilson found herself standing beside Dylan Walsh who was now back inside his own body. He started to speak.

"Is that why he was so angry?" Walsh asked innocently.

"Your father," the voice answered, "was once full of love and life. In an instant, however, sanity becomes insanity when the proper pressure is applied."

"So why didn't you stop him?" Walsh asked the voice.

"Because that is not what I wanted for man nor man wants for himself," the voice answered. "We are all guided by the decisions we make, but we are all free to make those decisions. I only offer forgiveness when the wrong decisions are made. I ask no questions. I just ask that you come to me with an open heart."

"That boy in the photo . . . is that him?" Peggy Wilson asked.

"Yes that is him," the voice answered. "His father should be more than familiar to you. "His father was the man you left behind that day . . . only much later in life. Love quickly turns to hate when left unchecked. Over the years hate grew into rage. Regardless of how he felt about being a father, he loved you. The girl who filled the void was a girl you once called your friend. She too was black. She was the object of his anger toward you and together they made a child. That child stands beside you now."

"The boy with the curly blond hair!" Peggy suddenly realized.

"I shaved it," he said holding back the tears, "because I didn't want to be like my father!" he added. "No one wants to grow up the bastard child of a Klansman and the town whore," he said fighting back the tears. "These tattoos are my way of reminding myself of how cruel life can be. I wrote HATE across my knuckles so that I could feel what it felt like to hate someone I didn't really know . . . each face I struck, I stuck for hate. The tattoo of the woman across my back is my mother. My father's face of hate is tattooed across my stomach . . ."

"But why didn't you reach out to . . ."

"The black community?" he answered with a question. "They were just as blinded by hate as the white community. You forget the "Black Nationalists" that roamed the streets following the bombing. They were convinced that the 'white' police wouldn't protect their little black children. I grew up in that community of hate. I grew up in the burned out cinders of that bombing. Every anniversary of the bombing was the anniversary of my conception. Every story on the news was a story about my father. There is no community for a child born of hate. The white community never knew of my existence. The black community didn't either. I wasn't black and I wasn't white and I wasn't wanted."

"So you shaved your head . . ."

"To hide my race and my shame," he answered.

Chapter thirty-seven

F ew noticed there was one person inside the holding room who had never uttered a single word. "Excuse me all you sinners," the rapper known as I-Hate began. "But what the hell am I doing here? I just wrote some rap songs and died in the wrong city at the wrong time. Judging from everything I've seen just standing here, you'll is one messed up group of people. I just wanted them to bury my ass so I can get to heaven or hell or where ever I'm going . . ."

"You will get there when I am ready for you to get there," the voice explained. "You were an entertainer. Like ministers and writers, you have the ability to affect the moods and behaviors of millions of people you never see. Because of that I show favor on the artists of the world. Your blessing is just that, a blessing. Your voice possesses power and therefore must be used wisely."

"But all I wrote was a bunch of songs," Hate countered.

"No, you wrote a bunch of songs to make money," the voice added.

"I remember you," Peggy Wilson said softly. "You used to sing in the youth choir before you went off and became all famous." She searched her memory. "Then it came to her. Isaiah Hawthorne!" she added. "I-Isaiah . . . Hate . . . Hawthorne . . . Rapper! You the one who spread all that filthy rap with all of those cuss words and all," she continued. "I'll bet your momma is ashamed of you!"

"I tell it like it is!" he answered defiantly. "I don't make this shit up. And I take good care of momma," he said.

"Watch your mouth boy," Peggy shot back.

"My bad ma'am," he said apologetically, an indication that he had been raised well. "What I rap about is history. I rap so that people never forget what happened to my people," he continued.

Virgil Thompson suddenly came back to life from his frozen form inside the holding room.

"What the hell is he doing here," Isaiah asked, face to face with the Klansman.

"He is here because of you," the voice added. "He is here because of you."

"I didn't nothing to do with him," I-Hate replied. "And I ain't taking the fall for all the shit that he did. I may have rapped about hate but I ain't responsible for all hate everywhere."

"No one is asking you to do so," the voiced said. "I am only asking you to take stock of that which *you* have done." As the voice spoke the room was filled with music. It wasn't the angelic type some believed associated with heaven. Instead it was rap.

"Is that what we're going to hear each day in heaven?" Virgil Thompson asked. "If so send me straight to hell anyway."

"That's my music," Isaiah Hawthorne said proudly. "I wrote that after them kids got killed in that bombing at that church. That's my music!"

Thompson replied angrily. "That's the song that that damned paramedic was listening to when he beat the crap out of me right before I died! I'd recognize that song anywhere."

"Serves your ass right!" Hawthorne added. "If that's the last song you heard before you died then you deserved it!"

"So now you are me?" the voice asked. "Now you get to decide who lives and who dies without consequence of your actions?"

"It's my fault," Peggy Wilson sobbed softly, but commanding the attention of all gathered. As she looked around she made sure to establish eye contact with all around her. Slowly she began to speak. "Without me, *none* of you would be here. *I* am responsible for the events that shaped all of your lives. I am the pebble in all of your ponds."

"And now you know the truth," the voice said softly. "The truth shall set you free."

And with those words, the rest of the room grew still. There was not a word to be spoken. A thunderous roar ripped across the holding room. It was as if there were an earthquake, and tornado occurring all at once. It was if the stone before the tomb of Jesus was being rolled back. God was about to pronounce judgment.

Chapter thirty-eight

When the thunderous roar stopped there was only silence . . . silence that was replaced by the cooing of a small child sitting naked in the corner. Instinctively Peggy Wilson walked across the room and stooped down to pick up the child and comforted him. "Who does he belong to?" she asked.

"He belongs to me," the voice answered. "All children do. For I have written that only the meek shall inherit the earth, and that only as a child will you enter into the kingdom of heaven. Each child is given a clean slate. It is what mankind does that shapes that child into what he or she grows up to be. The child you sacrificed might have discovered a cure for the cancer that ailed you. He might have bridged the racial divide that exists so deeply in your community."

"So now I understand why I will never go to the other side," she said apologetically. "I don't deserve to go to heaven . . ."

"Few do," the voice answered. "But that is not the test of who gets in and who stays here. This place is for us to learn about our sins before entering into heaven. It is the last stop for those who aren't quite ready to cross over. Look around you . . . this is what you didn't see."

Suddenly Peggy Wilson found herself inside the maternity room of Ohio Valley General Hospital. She felt sixteen. She examined her hands. She looked sixteen. She was herself, but in a different time and younger. In this version of her past she was surrounded by her parents and his parents. Unable to believe what she was seeing, her father began to explain, "We thought we lost you there for a while," he said.

"You should have told someone!" Her mother interrupted. "No *child* should bring a *child* into this world," she continued.

"Mr. Walsh?" she said unable to believe the fact that the man standing beside her, was known for his hatred. "What are *you* doing here?" she asked.

"We may not see eye to eye on a lot of things, but no Walsh ever walks away from his responsibilities," he said sternly. "My boy says he's the father of this child and I take em at his word for it. That means that baby you had is my flesh and blood. That means we're kinfolk."

Mrs. Walsh chimed in, "*We* take him at his word."

"That child don't deserve to be brought into a world of hate," her mother said entering the conversation. "Sent here from God to make sense of all this mess," she added. "We talked it out while you was in a coma. Been two weeks now . . . you was sleepin real good," she continued. "The two families will take turns raising the child so you two children can get a proper education. Seems that we're not that different after all when it comes to what we want for you two . . . what we want for our children."

The conversation was interrupted by a nurse who entered the room with the child in question. "She's a hell raiser," she said holding up a small child whose eyes seemed remarkably large. The face was innocent . . . angelic. "This little girl kept all the other kids up last night. Not to mention those diapers!"

The last remark prompted laugher from all around. Although un-quieting, and somewhat awkward, it was laughter none-the-less.

Then . . . as quickly as it began . . . it was over. The hospital room was no more. The parents were gone. There was no child. She was back inside the holding room again.

"It was a dream, wasn't it?" she asked.

"Not a dream," the voice answered, "but instead a parallel reality. I wanted you to see how life is full of possibilities. You have the ability to change the lives of so many around you. All of you did," the voice continued, motioning to the others around her. "None of your were ever alone. I was there by your side through each and every step. Life is to learn from. It is not the final stop on your journey but instead, the beginning of a long process. That process is far from over."

Without explanation, the darkness that filled the room was replaced by light. Everyone inside began to change. It was as if, in that moment, time stood still. Those who were old became young, and those who were young become older. Cars, houses, even animals aged before her very eyes. It was as if she were watching history unfold in a single moment.

"What's going on?" She asked.

"They're preparing to cross over," the voice answered. "They're getting ready."

"Even him?" she asked pointing to Virgil Thompson.

"Even him," the voice answered. "All are equal in the eyes of God," he continued.

As she watched the transformations started to make sense. The skinhead was now the curly haired little boy in the picture, full of life and innocence. Virgil Thompson was much younger as well, trying to wedge through the door of an abusive household, hoping to slip through the crevices of hate. The picnic went off as planned and the racial divides that separated a city healed much faster than anyone anticipated. There was no song for Isaiah Hawthorne to write about and no hate to spur it. Instead his father stood proudly by as his wife won the ribbon for the best pie that year at the Macedonia church picnic. The anger that guided their son was replaced by the music of the world's newest classical composure. Absent the stress, he lived much longer. The racial divide that separated the community paved the way for immigrants like Suleiman Muhammad to start not just one, but a string of hot dog restaurants up and down the valley. His name proudly graced the new athletic facility where all the kids played. He bought and paid for their uniforms.

All save one began to change. Reverend Kinney was still himself.

"Why isn't he changing?" Peggy Wilson asked.

"He will not be crossing over," the voice explained.

"Why? Were his sins so great?"

"No sins are too great, but his sins were different. Because he was a man of God, I hold Reverend Kinney to a much higher standard. I do so with all who take up the cross. The rest of you sinned out of ignorance and innocence. He did not, and therefore he will not be allowed to cross over . . . at least not yet."

"What about me?" Peggy asked.

"That's up to you. You have paid dearly for your sins and punished yourself with a lifetime of guilt. Like I said, I forgave you long ago. Did you forgive yourself?"

There was hesitation . . . followed by a stammer. "I might be able to forgive myself, but I have a favor to ask . . ."

"I know you are tired, my child, but there is one more thing you need to learn about the importance of where you are now," the voice interrupted. "You forget that I am Alpha and Omega . . . the beginning and the end. Therefore I am able to judge what has happened, and what is about to happen, but to change what appears to have happened as well . . . ."

"I don't understand . . ."

"You will," the voice replied. "But first there is one last piece of unfinished business."

Chapter thirty-nine

"Reverend Kinney?" the voice began.

By now the body of the deceased minister shuddered at the very mention of his name. "Please no more," he begged, to no avail. "I have seen enough," he pleaded.

"You have seen only how your actions affected your life," the voice replied. "These are the chapters in that book I left you that you somehow conveniently missed."

"But I read it from cover to cover," Reverend Kinney responded defiantly.

"But you did not understand it," the voice replied. "How about a quiz?"

"Quiz?"

"Yes," the voice began. "I will give you a chapter and verse, you tell me what it says."

"Okay . . ."

"John 14:2," the voice began.

"In my father's house there are many mansions," Reverend Kinney said proudly.

"And so my dear pastor, how many rooms have you seen so far?" the voice asked.

"Just this one," Reverend Kinney replied. "Just this one."

"Mark 10:25?'

"It is easier for a camel to pass through the eye of a needle than for an rich man to enter the gates of heaven," he said proudly.

"I see you are familiar with what the Bible says, but do you understand what it means?" the voice asked.

"That particular chapter seems to be self-explanatory," Reverend Kinney answered. "I preach from it often. It has to do with the vices of greed and lust for money," he added.

"And yet you stand before me guilty of that very sin," the voice replied. "Follow me. I want to show you another room I have assembled."

For the second time in what seemed to be a matter of seconds Reverend Kinney felt his knees begin to shake uncontrollably. "Is it another scene from my past?" he asked sheepishly.

"Not yours," the voice said, "but theirs."

Reverend Kinney found himself surrounded by men who appeared to be grossly obese. They more closely resembled bodies that spent days in the water before being discovered by authorities. He had presided over their funerals, and begged the families to close the caskets because they were too grisly to view. "What happened to these men?"

"You'll see. But first you have to walk through that," the voice answered.

"Step right up," a small man standing at the entrance to the room barked, in much the same manner he did in life at a carnival. "Pass through the eye of the needle and enter into the gates of heaven!" he shouted. "No one has managed to do so yet." And then with the slightest of a twinkle in his eye he motioned for Reverend Kinney to advance. "Do you think you'll be the first?"

Reverend Kinney watched as the obese men tried vainly to get through the eye of the needle but to no avail. "Why do they keep trying?" he asked.

"They keep trying because the other side of the needle is hell," the voice answered. "They have been here for an eternity."

"But why are they so fat?"

"Their weight is directly proportional to their wealth and what they did or didn't do with their money," the voice answered. "Most were men of great wealth who assembled fortune that could feed many small third world countries. Yet, rather than to do so, they simply chose to invent more ways to make more money. The more they made, the more they took away from someone else who desperately needed help," the voice continued. "I simply fed their appetite," the voice added sarcastically.

"How many rooms are there like this one?" Reverend Kinney asked.

"There are more rooms than the mind can count," the voice answered. "Further down the hall I have a room for women I call the "Salt Room"", the voice continued.

"Salt Room?"

"Yes it is a room for vain people, who because of their vanity couldn't resist a final look in the mirror," the voice began. "I simply gave them what they wanted."

"Salt?"

"No, one last moment frozen inside their own vanity," the voice answered.

In that instant the carnival barker disappeared and Reverend Kinney found himself surrounded mostly by women in various stages of pose. Each body glistened with the chrystaline glow of salt. One woman, who was completely nude, struck a pose in front of a bathroom mirror. Another caught a glimpse of her beauty in the rear view mirror of an auto.

'Watch this," the voice said.

Frozen no more, everything around the woman began to move, including a fast approaching car. Seconds later she was airborne.

"She failed to see the approaching danger because she could not take her eyes off of her own beauty," the voice said. "Had she been looking at something other than herself she would still be alive today."

"So are you saying that vanity and greed are as deadly as rape and murder?" Reverned Kinney asked.

"I am saying exactly that," the voice answered. "One leads to another. All wars are fought over money and wealth. Men have murdered because women chose to manipulate them because using their beauty . . . there was David and Beersheba, Samson and Delilah, and the list goes on throughout eternity. There is no such thing as one sin being more innocent than another."

Reverend Kinney reflected back on his own past, this time without having to journey back. He knew his sins and how he blindly pursued wealth and power by choosing to manipulate the very words of the Bible he preached from. "How much weight do I need to lose?" he asked.

"It no longer matters," the voice replied. "It is too late."

"Too late?"

"Matthew 12," the voice said sternly.

For the first time Reverend Kinney was stumped. "I don't understand," he said fearing his judgment was indeed upon him. "Matthew 12?"

"Verses 34 and 37," the voice answered. "I tell you that everyone will have to give account on the Day of Judgment for every empty word they have spoken . . ."

"But there still is time . . . ."

"For by your words you will be acquitted, and by your words you will be condemned."

With those words the bulbous men and the carnival barker were no more replaced by everything that slithered and swarmed. There were snakes as far as the eye could see, hundreds of thousands of snakes. Slowly they crawl across the feet of Reverend Kinney until he could no longer see the floor. He was engulfed. As they moved closer and closer he cried out, "Have mercy!" But it was too late.

"Matthew 12 verse 34," the voice answered. "You brood of vipers, how can you who are evil say anything good? For the mouth speaks what the heart is full of."

Then there was only silence, save the screams of a man who had just been sentenced to an eternity in hell.

Chapter forty

"We have breaking news . . ." the network news reporter began. He was surrounded by palm trees and looked to be standing in the courtyard of some Middle Eastern hotel. A fountain was positioned over his right shoulder and a palatial temple filled the rest of the frame. "There has been a strange twist in the Mideast peace process," he said fighting for breath. "Shortly after being taken to the hospital, following what was believed to have been a near fatal heart attack, the head of the Arab delegation demanded his release from the hospital," he continued. "I was told it was against doctor's orders," he added. "Sources close to the negotiations say he did so so that he could return to the peace process. He called it an *epiphany!*"

"Epiphany?" The anchor back in the studio asked. Placing his hand under his chin for emphasis he added, "I have heard a lot of rhetoric coming out of those talks but an 'epiphany'. Did he clarify?"

"Actually he did," the reporter answered starting to regain his composure. "He said there is something about a *brush with death* that caused him to take a second look at the life he was leading. That brush with death, he said, was what caused him to rededicate his belief that peace was actually possible. Then he said something else that left us all puzzled," the reporter continued. "He said sometimes achieving peace means seeing things from the perspective of your enemy . . . or as he put it, waking up with your enemy staring you in the face . . . and God as the referee. That, he said, was what he would bring back to the peace process."

"It almost sounds as if he is saying that he will be negotiating for the *other* side," the anchor said shifting nervously in his chair. As he spoke, a graphic seemed to appear over his shoulder out of nowhere. It read, "Peace in the Middle East?" The thought of actual peace in the Middle East seemed so remote, the phrase *conflict* and *Middle East* had become almost synonymous. For decades reporters came and went. One side threw stones, the other fired from the safety of tanks. Both sides claimed they were right. The irony was that they were fighting over the holy land.

"That is what I thought I heard him say," the reporter replied. "It seems that he is going to break with the rest of the delegation and take on the cause from a different perspective. He said something about . . . having a second chance at life . . . whatever that means."

"So the Arab is now going to argue form the Jewish perspective . . . what could possibly happen next?" the anchor asked sarcastically.

"How about peace?"

"That would be novel," the anchor remarked.

Chapter forty-one

The cameras came to life as the door opened and the wheelchair entered the room. The strobes from the hundreds of flashes going off gave the appearance of the surreal. The South L.A. Medical Center was known for its prowess in saving gunshot patients, but this patient was unlike any it had treated. Most of those served up on a gurney from the streets were gang bangers and illegal immigrants running from police. This man was different. This man was a celebrity. As a result, several reporters from the tabloids tried to ask questions before the rapper could speak but he waved them off with a slight flick of his wrist. He was rap royalty and he acted as such . . . until he spoke.

"I first want to thank God," he began much to the astonishment of the gathered throng of reporters. "Without him, I would be dead," he continued.

"*You* want to thank *God?*" a reporter asked.

The rapper known as "The Great White Hope" had a well known reputation for being an atheist who did not believe in

God and *did* believe in vengeance. His songs were filled with the venom of an artist who grew up on the other side of the tracks in Cleveland, where both sides battled to see who could be poorer. He wrote of anger, and violence, and hate. It appeared that he was going to die as he lived . . . violently. Doctors told reporters he had been shot so many times that they lost count of the bullets. In truth, there were ten. After two months in an induced coma, Hope was alive.

"But God?" another reporter continued.

"You got a better explanation for this?" Hope asked. "I mean look at me. I should be dead. Got more holes in me now than Swiss cheese," he added causing the gathered reporters to chuckle. "I overheard the paramedic telling the doctors in the ER that I was already DOA. He even said those letters, they sound so harsh now. Now I know . . . we ain't dead until God says we are dead . . ."

"Who shot you," a reporter interrupted. It had long been rumored that a rival gang in his hometown of Cleveland tracked him down in Los Angeles and opened fire. "Hope" however, was having none of it.

"I am responsible for what happened to me," "Hope" answered. "I ain't got nobody to blame by myself. Can't sing this shit and expect to live a long and health life . . ."

"You sound like you're a changed man," a tall blond reporter interrupted. It was clear from the way she flicked her hair back and forth that she was more interested in her looks than her questioning. "I mean . . ." she added for emphasis before being cut off in mid sentence.

"You ever been dead?' "Hope" asked. "I seen a lot of things when I was in that comma. It's like that movie "Eyes wide shut", only mine was wide open. You dream a lot when you're dead. I'm talking about bizarre dreams of heaven and hell. Stuff I don't never want to see again. And you hear a lot too. I heard it all. I heard the television in the corner of the room. I heard the doctors and nurses who came in my room and acted like I was dead already. They was saying that what happened to me was God's will and that I deserved to die. That's when you really find out what people think about you . . ."

"Will you go back into the recording studio?"

"Yes . . ." "Hope" began before adding a qualifier, "but not as "Hope" . . . let's just say I'm changing my style."

Again the cameras clicked widely as if capturing that moment was more important than the others. The flashbulbs created a strobe effect that seemed to follow "Hope's" every movement.

"So what will your new style be? Rap, R&B, soul . . ." another reporter asked.

"Hope" smiled. Then leaning forward against the table that sat directly in front of him he suggested, "Gospel!"

"Gospel?" a reporter asked almost reflexively. It was as if God had delivered the Ten Commandments. "I would have thought a lot of things . . . but Gospel?"

"Yeah and that ain't all," "Hope" answered. "Had a chance to look in the mirror of my own soul," he began. "Seems that God blessed me with a lot of things I took for granted. I used the gift of language and words to destroy, as opposed to build. I don't want to be "The great white hope" or anyone's hope for all that matters. I want to be an inspiration to people who need inspiring. So from here on out, I ain't going by the name of "The Great White Hope" no more," he answered. "My new name will just be "Hope!"

Chapter forty-two

This time Peggy Wilson watched it all unfold from the comfort of a cushioned recliner. Not surprisingly it was identical to the one she had in the TV room of her old house with her daughter. She was starting to understand the secrets of the holding room. It fed on fears, and hope, and love. It also fed on a simple principle. Ask not . . . get not. She realized that God was the voice inside her head, feeding on her fears and rewarding her desires. She asked for a recliner and got the Cadillac of comfort chairs, just as was the case in her life. She figured if she was going to spend an eternity watching life unfold, she might as well be comfortable.

"So people's spirits come and go?" Peggy Wilson asked as she watched life on the world stage as God does.

"Sometimes people need another shot at life," the voice answered. "The fear of death and an eternity in hell is an incredible motivator. People waste their entire lives only to find *life* in the seconds before death. Such was the case with "Hope" whom I think you might recognize as one of your friends here in the holding room, or that Arab negotiator in the Mid—East peace process. I allowed them all to go back and make a few amends before returning to the holding room for their final judgment. But make no mistake about it, the other side works just as hard to turn people the other way. It is a constant battle . . . this battle between heaven and hell."

"But Reverend Kinney took the place of a man who people loved . . . ."

"Sometimes a person's life on earth has been completed. When that happens, as was the case with Pastor Graham, I allow them to come straight home. Because he had already removed himself from society it was okay to remove him. Because he was in Africa, no one will notice that the man who took his place has a pretty steep learning curve. They will chalk it up to shell shock at first. Sooner or later, Revered Kinney will come to accept the fact that he is Pastor Graham."

"So he died . . ."

"Death is such a *human* term. We have an eternity to spend in heaven. Don't you think it would get kinda boring just sitting around on clouds playing harps?" Once again there was a hint of sarcasm in the voice. "The music alone would be monotonous, although I have to admit the *other side* invented rap. I-hate it . . . get it? I-Hate it? There are so many problems that can be solved on earth; the best among you go back again and again to fix things in my name . . ."

"So this may not be my first visit to the holding room?"

"No . . . in fact you have been here several times over the ages. Many of those I have sent back have become some of the greatest names in human history. I believe you call it déjà vu," the voice answered. "Some become what you would call "prodigies." Imagine a second chance at life for people who were given great gifts but wasted them the first time around. People like the basketball player who succumbed to drugs, or the musician who died in a car accident. Once you conquer your fear of death and truly realize *what* it takes to get into heaven, life becomes more enjoyable," the voice added. "People like you, who get to the holding room and now say they want to *stay,* are unusual. In fact I can think of only one such case. I don't usually get that too often, at least not when they get here."

"Is that true with . . ."

"The baby . . ."

"Yes."

"I have plans for the baby," the voice answered. "I always do."

"Can I see those plans take shape?" Peggy Wilson asked. "I lost a child once and would just once like to know what it feels like to see that child grow up," she said softly. "I know now that I lost a very special child," she added. "I now know that all children are special."

"We'll see what can be done. I know people in *high* places," the voice answered.

Then for the first time since she was in the holding room, Peggy Wilson could have sworn she heard God laugh.

"First," he began. "Follow me!"

Chapter forty-three

"Open the door," the voice said softly.

Fear flooded Peggy Wilson's spirit. Even though she was certain she had spent only an instance in the holding room, she had learned quickly that behind each door in our lives there are there are the unforeseen consequences of our lives. This door, she expected, would be no different. "What's on the other side?" she asked softly.

"You destiny," the voice explained. "There is nothing to fear. You have chosen to remain behind, but in doing so; you will also need a place to stay. The holding room is not a prison. For each person who enters and exits, their time spent here is a small fraction of the eternity they will spend in the afterlife." Then pointing toward the door, he added, "Please feel free to go inside."

The door slowly began to open, almost as if responding to her thoughts and not her touch. Peggy Wilson couldn't believe her eyes. The first thing she noticed was the smell, an exquisite fragrance unlike anything she had ever experienced. It smelled of the best perfumes all mixed into one large bottle. There were plants, all of them exotic, unlike any she had ever seen. Towering redwoods gave way to palm trees and foliage from various climes. There were animals, thousands upon thousands of animals, all roaming free in apparent harmony. There was the lion and the lamb, literally sitting down together. And there were children, of all shades and nationalities, laughing and playing. The young and the not so young frolicking as far as the eye could see.

"I've never seen anything like it," she said.

"Nor will you ever," the voice answered. "The finest quill cannot capture the true beauty of nature. Man's best brushstroke always has flaws that can always be seen upon closer examination. Perfection leaves nothing to question, therefore when the horizon meets the land in life it is seamless. This is the world as I created it in the Garden of Eden. It is perfect harmony. There is no pollution to fowl the air, or skyscrapers to block your view. You will hear no autos or sirens or honking horns . . . just the song of the birds as they serenade all who chose to listen. There are no cell phones in heaven."

As her eyes scanned the horizon, she spotted a rainbow but like the children it was anything but ordinary. Every shade, every hue in the rainbow . . . seemed alive! The blues were the brightest blues she had ever seen and the yellows were unlike anything on earth. It was like the box of crayons she had as a child. First there were five colors, and then as she grew older, sixty four. There were interwoven tones of orange and red and green that seemed to give the rainbow life. "That is the most beautiful rainbow I think I have ever seen," she remarked.

"That is because it is not any ordinary rainbow," the voice answered. "Watch."

As she watched the rainbow appeared to move, bending and reshaping itself in one fluid motion. It was as if her own thoughts controlled the pattern. With each shifting wave the rainbow seemed to grow larger until it appeared to gather itself and move toward her. As the rainbow moved closer she realized it was not a rainbow but, "Butterflies?"

"Keep watching . . ."

Closer still the rainbow arched and swayed from side to side, in a sea of blue and black and yellow butterflies, with paler shades of gray and green she assumed to be Luna moths. As it moved even closer she realized there were more than butterflies making up the rainbow. The brighter shades of yellow were exotic canaries; the reds were cardinals brighter than she had ever seen, with blue birds and blue jays complimenting the butterflies filling in the spectrum of beauty. Side by side with the Luna moths were green canaries that she had seen once in a brochure from some far away island. There were millions of them, the butterflies, the birds, and the beauty of nature in one single symphony. "Is this heaven?"

"No . . . you are still in the holding room, but it is a different room. You see, in my house . . ."

"There are many mansions . . ."

"I see that that you did more with that book than to let it collect dust on your mantle," the voice replied sarcastically. "Yes there are many rooms in this place but this is the most precious of all . . ."

"Is it because of the children?" Peggy Wilson looked around and saw small children as far as she could see. There was wave upon wave of children, playing and frolicking as if they had no cares whatsoever. There were black children side by side with white children, Muslims with Christian children and Asians playing alongside whoever was closest. ". . . there are so many"

"And each is very very special . . ."

Her face saddened. "They have no parents," she said, looking around and seeing none. The sight of seeing so many small children with no parental involvement was both innocent and unusual and sad. "It is as if they were all . . ."

"Abandoned? They were," the voice replied. "You are very perceptive Peggy Wilson. They are children, who by no fault of their own never had the heaven on earth that so many take for granted. Their parents died in wars, or from starvation or poverty. They are the children of Africa, South America, Asia and parts of Europe who died or starved to death in the most horrible of manners. Their parents died from bullets supplied by other, more prosperous countries. They starved in a world where there is an abundance of food. Do not think that I have not seen the hypocrisy. People on one continent starve, while those a half a world away battle obesity . . ."

"And wars . . ." Her mind raced back to the many images she had seen on the evening news or splashed across the front pages of the newspapers she cherished. There were too many conflicts to count and so like many she stopped counting and caring.

"Think of how it sounds . . . a child soldier. War in itself is bad enough, but to use children as fodder for the folly of man sickens me to the core. These children were too young to understand the consequences of their actions that were ordered by adults who did. They were handed weapons and told to kill. It is the most horrible of circumstances anyone can image. That is why they are here. They needed shelter from the storm of the world that you created . . . ."

Peggy remembered one photograph in particular. She remembered the image of a small child holding and loading a rifle that was larger than he. "Are they going to be here . . . ?"

"Forever? Oh heaven's no," the voice answered. "They would have gone straight to heaven but they weren't ready yet. Many are from parts of the world where starvation is the norm, or war is commonplace. To get to heaven would be too much too soon. It would be too much of a shock. Here they can laugh and play until I have deemed the time is right. There they will spend an eternity in much the manner you see before you, only better . . . ."

"Is that snow?" she asked, startled to see the white stuff falling from the sky, while the temperature inside the room seemed to be tropical.

"Snows here every day," the voice answered. "Although I have to admit that the snow and cold was a mistake on my part. A day here is a year in your world. These children have years of life to live before they are ready to go onto the next step so I sped up the calendar. Each and every day these children experience all four seasons. It keeps things from getting boring . . . ."

"Snowball fights . . ." she said as she watched a small child holding a bolder of a snowball about to launch it.

"Every day . . . ."

"It smells like . . ."

"Hamburgers today," the voice began as if reading a mental menu. "Hamburgers today followed by French fries for lunch. Earlier they had sliced bacon . . . as much as they could eat atop a sea of eggs. That's the best part of being here, no cholesterol."

"The area almost smells like a carnival midway," Peggy Wilson added. "It has that feeling of endless fun about it . . ."

"And that's the way it is supposed to be," the voice replied. "These children never knew the joy that so many children take for granted. It is written that to enter into the kingdom of heaven, we must see the world through the eyes of a child. These children were robbed of that very small privilege and so here, they can find out what it is like to never have a care in the world."

Peggy took a deep breath, smelling air that for the first time in her life was free of pollutants. There was nothing in the way of anything foul. It was as if she woke up in the mountains, and then strolled over to the ocean and fell asleep under the moonlit sky. As she thought it, it became real. Each time she blinked the landscape changed. She opened her eyes and saw before her a mountain of such grandeur it could not belong to earth. At its base the waves of a crystal blue ocean lapped in a rhythmic motion that was both soothing and seductive. "What are those sounds?" she asked. It sounded as if a full symphony were playing and yet there were no instruments to be seen.

"In heaven, when you are the conductor, it is amazing what you can do with life's symphony," the voice answered. "The wings of a butterfly make no sound, when measured against the rush of the everyday hustle and bustle, and yet here, when combined with the multitudes that have come and gone before you they created my bass. The drones of locusts are my violins. Theirs is a tone that not even the most accomplished virtuoso can reproduce. The lions roar and bring to life my baritones. Together they will join together and create the music life was meant to enjoy. They will sing the songs of life. So you see . . . all things really do come together for the good of God."

Peggy could not take her eyes off the scene unfolding before her. The floor of the room was filled with colors, brighter and bolder than she had ever seen before. They weren't just the colors she had grown accustomed to seeing, but, instead, shades she had not yet seen. The sky above was blue, but various shades of blue. The same was true of the grass and the waves that crashed in from the ocean which whipped up against a multi color sand beach. Not far from where the beach met the water, were plants and different foliage that defied explanation. "What are these?" she asked stooping over to pull one closer, but not daring to pick it.

"I believe it is what you call *weeds,*" the voice answered.

"All of these?" she asked. Surveying the landscape she realized that she did not see a single flower she recognized. Instead there was a pallet of colors, so bold, and so brilliant, all painted by the plants that so many for so long have taken for granted. There in the middle of it all, swaying back and forth in the gentle breeze, was her favorite, Ironweed. A single stalk rose majestically from the ground, topped by a flowering array of purple flowers. "They *are* weeds," she said excitingly. ". . . but why?"

"This room is for all of those things that are lost. Everything in this room has been discarded by society. It was once written that weeds are a flower by any other name. Who is to say that the rose is beautiful, and yet the dandelion is not? Have you ever seen a field full of dandelions in spring, after the winter has made its exit? Because of your categories, your constant need to separate, earth becomes ugly. It is as if there was something that I placed on earth by mistake . . ."

As she made her way through the garden, she realized the ground beneath her feet began to make a crunching sound. "Hail?"

"Exactly. I call it the perfect gardener. All of nature needs pruning. In times of extreme drought, the rains would wash away everything in its path. I use hail to clear away the smaller dead branches and leaves on trees that would normally wait until fall to drop to the ground. Rain nourishes, hail clears, making for smaller particles that then wind up being what you would call . . . mulch."

The further she walked the more she realized that, nothing on earth was a mistake. In a matter of hours she watched as winter gave way to spring, and spring to summer and summer to fall. She began to reflect back on her favorite bible verse, Matthew six, "*behold the lilies of the field how they neither toil nor sew and yet Solomon in all his glory were not as arrayed as these*." There before her, was what appeared to be heaven. A heaven filled with animals that seemed to frolic openly with the children in fields filled with what she once considered weeds. It was the most beautiful sight she had ever seen. "Are there animals in heaven?"

"There are more than the eye can count," the voice replied. "These, however, aren't any ordinary animals."

Chapter forty-four

Peggy wanted to know more. "They look ordinary," she said softly referring to the large collection of animals that seemed to assemble before her.

"They are far nobler than that," the voice replied. "All of these animals once roamed free, without worry. But in your world they died along the highways and roadways. Most were not afforded the dignity of a gentle death and instead were left along those same roadways to rot. And yet each of these animals served a special role in the way the world is shaped . . ."

"I don't understand?"

"Nor would you know that . . . unless you really did understand that that all things work together for the good of God," the voice answered. "Each of those animals sacrificed their lives for someone to live. Man is so self-centered that he cannot see the bigger picture unfolding around him. How many times have you left your house only to forget your keys?" the voice asked. "Then you return home, get back in your car and go about your merry way. It isn't until you get further down the road that you realize that had you continued . . . had you not lost that set of keys . . . you would have been in a massive accident further down the road . . . ."

"Serendipity . . . it happens all the time . . ."

"And yet you never ask why?" the voice said. "These animals sacrificed their lives for the greater good. They realized the dangers in the road up ahead and ran into that road so that others, who had larger roles to play in my larger plan, might live. This is their reward. The forest is filled with the smaller saplings that gladly sacrifice their lives for the animals that they see as heroes. Here those saplings are in turn surrounded by the flowers that decorate their world, and the children who see them through eyes of wonderment. Unlike the zoos of your world, there are no cages or bars to contain them. They are free to come and go as they please . . . ."

"There are no adults here," Peggy Wilson said as she continued to try and make sense of everything thing around her. "Why?"

"I created man in my own image, and gave him dominion over all of this. That is the gift I bestowed upon you on earth," the voice began by way of explanation. "It was all there and yet because of your greed, your lust for more, you do not see the simplest blessings before you. Children do. How many times have you seen a child play for hours with their shadows, or marvel at the inner workings of an ant hill . . ."

"We miss so much . . ."

"You see what you choose to see. That is why for man, there is heaven *and* hell. Without the possibility of something far better, or far worse, man would simply consume. You would take and take until there was no more. You would destroy yourselves . . ."

"So most people either wind up in one of those two places?"

"Most . . . but not all," the voice added. "Other's I call *"pass throughs"* They are good people who live just lives and therefore go straight to heaven to be reunited with their loves. There is also the holding room where, like you, they wait to be judged. Few, in fact, none who has ever made it to the holding room has ever chosen to stay here. Most can't wait to get to heaven. None wishes to go to hell, but that is understandable . . ."

"So you're saying that I am the first . . ."

"You are the first person who has ever chosen to stay behind. The door to heaven is on the other side of *this* room. It is on the other side of that mountain and across that ocean. You are free to enter into heaven anytime you chose. All you have to do is knock . . . ."

"Knock and the doors shall be opened . . . seek and ye shall find . . ."

"No, actually just knock on the door and someone will let you in," the voice answered the hint of sarcasm returning. "Just knock."

"And the children?"

"These children are happy here," the voice answered. "They too will one day cross over into heaven once they realize that there is a kinder world out there, than the one they have known their entire lives. Each has a special place in my heart, and each will have a special place in my kingdom. You will be more than welcome here until you are ready to make the passage home."

"I don't think I'll ever leave," Peggy Wilson added.

"There is one last thing I want to show you," the voice added. "I suspect once you see it you will change your mind. Remember, there are thousands of your loved ones waiting for you in heaven. There are those who went on before you and those who will follow you. I suspect it is the latter you will look forward to seeing."

"How do I get there?"

"How about you put your heels together . . . and click them three times . . ."

"I get it . . . there's no place like home," she replied smiling.

Chapter forty-five

As the door to the last room opened, Peggy Wilson heard the muffled cries of people crying. The room smelled of suntan oil and the endless summer. As she tried to process the scene before her, she tried to make sense of the tears. The people who filled the room seemed to be in perfect health. Their bodies were tan and fit and most looked like they had just emerged from a workout session in the gym. Each wore the uniform of their day. One woman wore leg warmers, while another man stationed right beside her wore spandex shorts that revealed far too much. All spent more time wiping away tears than anything else. "Why are these people crying?" she asked.

"They are in the prime of their lives," the voice replied.

"I don't understand?"

"Neither did they," the voice added. "They are trapped in what they believed to be the perfect moment. Each person, at one time or another, wished for the life that now lies before them . . . a life, that they believed to be . . . perfect."

"So what happened?"

"It's actually kind of high tech. Take a look at their exercise bikes."

Peggy Wilson walked across the room realizing that not one of the bikes was in use. The same was true of the weight machines and the recumbent bikes that seemed to stretch for miles.

All of them, perfectly sound exercise equipment, all sitting idle. As she walked closer she realized that each piece of equipment was outfitted with small video monitors which cast an eerie bluish glow over the room. "Do these work?" she asked.

"All too well," the voice answered. "Take a closer look."

As she glanced into the monitors each one played a different scene. One showed a family at Christmas, with small kids under the tree opening their gifts. Another monitor showed a family on a vacation at the beach. A little boy raced back and forth trying not to get wet by the waves of the ocean. His parents were never far away, just in case something went wrong. Stretched out on a blanket, was an elderly couple that seemed to be soaking in more than the sun. As she approached a monitor on the recumbent bike she saw a birthday party. From the candles on the cake, it was clear that it was the first birthday of the little girl who wondered what all of the commotion was about. Surrounding the cake were her parents with the child's grandparents in tow complete with cameras to capture the moment. The more she saw, the more she wondered why those in the room seemed to be so upset.

"I don't understand," she began. "These scenes are so happy, so cheerful, and so full of life, why are these people so upset?" she asked.

"They are upset," the voice began by way of explanation, "because the events unfolding on the monitors are the lives they left behind. Life, like the days and nights that comprise it, is made up of seasons. There is a season for youth, a season for teenage angst and anger, a season to replant and a season to soak in the harvest. Each season is as important as the one before it. These people, as all do, believe that the season that they were living in was the best . . ."

"Is anything wrong with that?"

"There is nothing wrong with believing that now is the best time of your life. That is the way I planned it. Where we go wrong, is dreading the next phrase. Young people look upon their parents as old, until they become parents. Parents look upon the years where their children are young as the best years of their lives, until they become grandparents. Grandparents often fear death, because . . ."

"They don't believe . . ."

"Precisely . . . they don't believe in life *after* death. The group of people you see before you reached that pinnacle in life and began to fear death more than they enjoyed living life. They mourned the loss of their youth and could only see the negative in growing old. They saw the lines in their faces and spots on their hands. They felt themselves slowing down, but failed to realize the reason for doing so. Had they seen what you have seen, they would have understood that *life* is just the beginning. There is so much more for the world of the faithful. What they see in the monitors is what they would have seen had they lived long enough. They see their grandchildren, and in some cases great grandchildren . . ."

"Will they ever get to heaven?" Peggy Wilson asked.

"They will, but there is a mourning period to go through first. Like all things, youth was never meant to be coveted, neither was parenting. When parents baptize their children they acknowledge that they are gifts. Few, however, actually believe that. Instead they believe that children are possessions . . . smaller versions of themselves if you will. As a result, they fail to fully realize the potential of parenting. Imagine what would have happened if Joseph and Mary had focused more on their lives than the life of the child they reared . . . ."

"There would have been no Christ child . . ."

"Man does not determine the seasons or the length of his life. Only God can do so. He is to live each day as if it is his last. Instead, we become obsessed with youth. We forget what we say when we grow older, that youth is wasted on the young. We also forget that your days on the earth when measured against the calendar of eternity are but a fraction of a second in the clock of life. You watched that clock in your room each and every morning waiting until the day of your death. I was there each and every second watching you watch your life . . ."

"I wasted it . . ."

"No . . . no life is ever wasted. It takes a fraction of a second for an auto accident to claim a life, or for a person the swerve to avoid it. Each life offers its own lessons. That is what makes man unique. In a planet of billions of people, each man and woman has their own special set of circumstances. No two of you are created alike. Like the individual snowflake in a blizzard, each fits into a grand mosaic that only I can see," the voice said.

Then the crying stopped! The music was no more. The silence was unnerving in itself. Slowly, in unison, all of those inside the room turned and faced Peggy Wilson.

"Why are they looking at me?" she asked.

"Because *your* monitor is now playing," the voice replied. "Perhaps you should take a look."

Slowly, Peggy Wilson walked over to a treadmill that showed her own life playing out in slow motion. On the screen, she recognized many of the episodes she wanted to remember, and many she wanted to forget. Finally she reached the end of what she remembered, but the monitor didn't stop. Instead, it continued playing. They were the moments just before her death. The second hand on the clock opposite her bed began its movements and life was renewed. But everything seemed unfamiliar. I don't recognize any of this," she said.

"That is because it is your future . . ."

"But there is a birthday celebration for a small child. All of my children are grown . . ."

"It is not your child," the voice answered. "It is your grandchild. It is the grandchild that was born after your death."

"That's impossible . . ."

"By now you should realize that nothing is impossible. Look closer at the celebration. Pay special attention to the cake."

Peggy Wilson looked down at the monitor. The parents celebrating the birthday were her youngest daughter, "Little Peggy" and her husband. They seemed so happy. The little girl seemed so full of life. Did they adopt?"

"They didn't have to."

Chapter forty-six

"Little Peggy" decided to leave Wheeling, and was making her way north toward Pittsburgh. Because of Suleiman Muhammad, the memorial service was a bust and, when the FBI finished its investigation, there was little interest in any funeral. Still, there was a small get together of family and friends, followed by a wake, with the obligatory food, which was enough to lay her mother to rest with proper honors. "It was," she told those gathered, "a celebration of the life of a good woman. Her mother," she explained, "was now in a better place walking side by side with her master." Most stayed until the last morsels macaroni and fried chicken were consumed and then left. Noticeably missing was anything in the way of leftovers. Those dishes that were brought to the wake made it back home in the same dishes that carried them to the wake . . . times being what they were and all.

The shadows of sporadic buildings and looming mountains danced on her windshield as she made her way out of town on I-70. The rhythm of the white lines in the road was hypnotic.

Looking down, she clutched the small brass Urn that contained her mother's ashes. "Where do you think she would like her ashes to be spread?" she asked her husband who was behind the wheel.

He paused for a moment before answering. "Somewhere near the church, perhaps in that garden they were putting together," he answered. He remembered his mother-in-law spending countless hours tilling the soil. He also remembered how she took care of the memories of those who had gone on before her. A small bench marked their membership and contribution. She was God's constant gardener.

"Any church but *that* church," "Little Peggy" replied, thinking of the scene that had just played out. "Too many painful memories there," she added.

"Your mother spent her life inside that church," her husband answered. "That's the problem with us church folk, we want to blame God for the things that man done wrong," he added. "You have to take the good with the bad when it comes to church folks. Remember there was Jesus and Judas . . ."

"I supposed you're right," she replied. "Still it just seems so . . ."

"Awkward!"

There was a pregnant pause and then both shared a laugh before moving on to more pressing matters. They started talking about what they would like for dinner. The I-70 corridor between Wheeling and Pittsburgh was a hodgepodge of ethnic

America. The food varied with each exit. The small town known as Little Washington was straight ahead, and like most of western Pennsylvania it was well known for its Italian food, but within a matter of a few minutes food was the last thing on "Little Peggy's" mind. Instead she felt like she wanted to vomit.

"John?"

"What is it?" he answered.

"I think I'm going to be sick," she replied. "Must have been something I ate at the wake. Probably Aunt Gwen's deviled eggs," she added, prompting even more laughter, before taking on a more serious tone. "But really, I think I'm going to throw up!"

John pulled off the interstate getting as close to the guard rail as he could. Before the car could come to a complete stop, the door swung open and "Little Peggy" leaned out of the passenger side seat and removed any doubt that there once were deviled eggs once inside her stomach . . . but no more.

After what seemed to be an eternity of rctching, John broke the silence. "Feel better?" He asked innocently, while at the same time wiping the perspiration away as it dripped from his wife's forehead. "Since when have you had problems eating anything?"

"I don't know what's come over me," she answered. "That's the second time today. I didn't want to say anything earlier, but when I woke up this morning I felt the same way."

Then they looked at each other and almost in unison uttered the same word . . .

"Nooo Waaaay!!!"

"That would be impossible," "Little Peggy" added. "I'm too old!" she added. *"Way too old!"*

"Remember Sarah in the bible?" John answered jokingly. "She thought she was too old too . . ."

"Remember Aunt Sarah from the funeral?" "Little Peggy" fired back, thinking of the wrinkled old lady who sat in the front row. "She *is* too old and so am I!"

Chapter forty-seven

Tears welled in the eyes of Peggy Wilson, as she watched it all unfold. Her mind raced back to the echoes of the baby that once kicked inside her. Like all things in her past, she now knew it never really went away. "Is that *the* baby?" she asked fearing the answer.

"It is," the voice explained. "Like everything else you have seen, you perhaps better than most, know that nothing is a mistake. I had plans for the child the moment you chose to let it go . . . you see . . . you are both my children. I trust you will believe me when I say it will be in good hands."

"They have been trying for so long," she added. "For so long they thought . . ."

". . . that they could not get pregnant," the voice answered. "So many times in past people have given up on their dreams only to find them at the last possible moment. If all miracles were possible . . . there would be no room for faith. Faith is the belief in things unseen."

"But she is so . . ."

"Is she older than Abraham and Sarah . . . or for that matter your own aunt Sarah who gave birth in her fifties?"

"They are going to be so happy," Peggy Wilson answered joyously. For the first time in years she wanted to dance. She wanted to shout her joy unto the heavens, she wanted to give thanks. "They will be perfect parents . . ."

"This is the way it should be . . ."

"That baby will be raised in love and happiness and will go on to do great things . . ."

"You mean the baby that bears *your* name," the voice replied.

"I thought that baby was a little boy?"

"You're child was. As I told you, nothing happens without being part of the much larger plan. There is never a time that a child is not a blessing, only the circumstances surrounding its birth. At times the world seems like it is coming to an end. The skies grow dark and rains fall, but then the heavens open up to produce a rainbow in colors bolder and brighter than anyone can imagine. I send you example after example of the miracles of life and yet time and time again you forget. Then you have to be reminded again."

"We are only . . . ."

"Human?"

"Yes . . . ."

"That is what makes you so much a part of my heart. I made you imperfect so that you might understand just a little of what it is like to be me. Perfection is a destination not a goal. The more things that go wrong, the more right we become. It is perhaps the greatest mystery of life. That is why we learn from our mistakes, more so than our triumphs. Man was never meant to be perfect . . . only God."

"The kingdom of God is within us," Peggy whispered.

"That is the way it was meant to be," the voice answered. "You always have the answers before you. The truth exists in your heart. Every little child is born with an innate sense of right and wrong. There is no longer a need for stone tablets and proclamations from a burning bush. I wrote those laws in your heart. When you abandoned your child you knew it was wrong and spent a lifetime paying for your sins . . ."

"I should have listened to my . . ."

"Heart . . . easier said than done when you are an unwed teenage mom living in a time of segregation. It is hard enough to bring a child into this world when all is well, let alone under times of extreme hardship. I understood . . . ."

"Thank you . . ." Peggy said as her voice trailed off into a sea of tears.

"You are forgiven."

They were the three words she had waited a lifetime and now death time to hear . . . three words so simple, and yet to powerful. Glancing down at the scene that played out on the monitor she knew God had indeed listened to her prayers, as the last one was being answered. The baby that she had abandoned now had a home . . . a loving home. She had but one last request.

"Father," she said politely. "Can I?"

"Yes . . ." he answered. "Yes you can," he added. "But there is one last thing you should see."

At that moment, the walls of the holding room suddenly opened up. Gone was the darkness as the room was flooded with light. The events unfolding were so real, that Peggy Wilson felt she could actually touch them. She was once again looking at the future, but not her own. Instead it was the future of the small child, her grandchild.

"Unlike you, your daughter believed in miracles and prayed for one each and every day. Even when her husband gave up, she didn't. She continued to pray in places where he could not see her. What you are looking at is the miracle they prayed for . . . . ."

Peggy Wilson couldn't take her eyes off the little girl in the monitor. She seemed so perfect, so at peace. She smiled as a pair of perfectly formed hands played with the icing, before making their way to her mouth. As Peggy Wilson looked closer, she saw it. The name on the cake . . . was hers! "They really did name the baby after me?"

"You thought I lied to you," the voice replied jokingly. "I never lie. I can't."

Then the pictures in the monitor changed. The events of the little girl's life played out in fast forward, as if controlled by a remote control. There she was riding a bike, on her first date, graduating from high school, and then from college. The little girl was now an adult.

"She's beautiful!"

"Her mother says she has your eyes and his personality," the voice answered. "I have big things in store for that child . . . very big things. You can watch the rest from heaven."

Peggy Wilson was overwhelmed. She had finally heard the words that proved God really had given her a second chance and opened the doors to heaven. "Heaven?"

"Yes heaven. Heaven will be a far better place for you. This place is for people who are not yet ready to cross over. You are no longer that person. It is time . . ."

Glancing around her one last time, Peggy Wilson took stock of the holding room. The souls that seemed so lost an eternity ago all found forgiveness in the eyes of a forgiving God. The room was empty. She recognized the voice as the conscious that had been there to guide her throughout her life. It controlled her thoughts and every movement. She realized in that moment, that had she followed the voice, her life would have been perfect. Still, following something as simple as a voice inside your head seemed so difficult during tough times. That's when she realized what faith was all about. It was about following that inner compass inside your head, even when it seemed counter to everything around you. Now the voice was speaking to her once again.

It was time.

It was right.

Time of departure, 9:30 am and a few odd seconds . . . it mattered little.

Epilogue

T hree things in life are certain, death, taxes and our time in the holding room.

My father used to tell me that his yesterday's far outnumbered his tomorrow's. I know now that he was wrong . . . not about life, but about death. We spend our entire lives thinking that once we die, it is all over. We pour into churches, listen to preachers, and talk a good talk, but when all is said and done, do we *really* believe? What happens *after* life falls into that tricky, murky, area called faith.

We celebrate Easter Sunday and the resurrection but in the back of our minds there is always that lingering doubt. We believe only what we see. Faith dictates that we believe in things unseen which, in this case, is an afterlife that no one has ever returned from. On that note it is important to consider the alternative.

What if death is not the end but, instead, the beginning of a long journey that will last through eternity? What if that second on a clock that we watch tick by, is a year or a decade or a century. And even then, what if it's . . . dying that is . . . is all contrary to what we've been taught to expect? What if there are no bright lights that we walk into once exiting our existing lives thinking we have become part of the celestial universe of the afterlife? What if we've been misled?

On one side of that argument, we have been told time and time again that there is heaven in all its glory. In heaven we are supposed to be greeted by a man who looks like a combination of Santa Clause and Socrates, who is full of wisdom and forgiveness. He speaks with a voice we all understand in dulcet tones that sooth our restless souls. To get to heaven we have become convinced that we will ascend a large staircase lined with the angels and harps that ends in the clouds where we will spend eternity with the same people we couldn't stand on earth. In heaven, we are told, there is no stress or strain, or arguments for that matter. No one hungers or thirst for anything, or has want or need.

By sharp contrast, on the other side, there is the inferno we have come to know as hell . . . the elevator south, Hades the gates of delirium. There, we are told, we will spend the rest of eternity, toiling under a horned being known as Satan, who legend has it, was once one of God's angels until they had a falling out. Hell is described as a prison, where people spend an eternity engulfed in constant flames, while evil eats at our every souls. Most of the people we *don't* want to see, will wind up there which is why some believe hell *is* on earth. They're closer to the truth that you might imagine.

In order to gain entry to either location, you first have to die and that's where things get murky. There is a process to get into heaven which is described in various literatures as judgment day, or the Day of Atonement. On that day, we are told, we will come face to face with God and each of our sins will be placed before us. Imagine being held accountable for every second, of every day, of every year of our lives . . . the good, the bad and the indifferent. How many of us would pass that test.

Sadly, that is the version of events that is much closer to the truth.

For you see, there not only is a heaven, and a hell, but a place in the middle. It is a place where we all will be judged. That place is what God calls the holding room. For as the bible says, in that house, "there are many mansions".

Del Walters has written seven books. His first fiction book, The Race, was prominently featured on Hardball with Chris Matthews during the 2008 election, as it accurately predicted the rise of the nation's first black president. The Holding Room is his sixth work of fiction. He is an Emmy Award winning news anchor, filmmaker and author who lives in the suburbs of Washington, D.C.